P.

Watermelons and Thistles

"As the son of a Norwegian immigrant father (and full Norwegian on my mother's side, too), I absolutely loved reading these memories of fellow Dakotans whose ethnic German people came to the prairie from the steppes of Russia. They may have preferred halupsie and *kuchen* to lutefisk and lefse, but the stories of farm chores and barn dances, church and one-room school, wash days and farm auctions, fighting prairie fires and thistle all ring true and honest and warmly, wonderfully human. The frustrations of genealogy and the exhilaration of discovery, the pride and the sadness that comes with knowing, are here and will be recognized and felt by people of all ethnic backgrounds who have searched for a better understanding of those who came before them."

Chuck Haga, University of North Dakota media writing instructor and former writer for the *Star Tribune* (Minneapolis-St. Paul)

"I laughed a little. I cried a little. I reminisced, thinking, "I remember my mom talking about that!" This collection made daily life in the German-Russian triangle of the Dakotas come alive for me. Spanning the years from when church and community were our families' whole world to the time when radio, TV, and war brought the outside world closer, these stories are delightful (and often poignant) reminders of our heritage."

Carolyn Schott, founder of the Black Sea Germans Research Community and author of *Visiting Your Ancestral Town*

"The past often seems friendlier from the perspective of the present. Old wounds heal, ruined structures decay or are forgotten, detritus washes down gullies of the mind. Memory heals and wrongs may be righted. Even the Great Depression loses its sharpest edges. The essays collected in this volume attest a life now named "heritage." It quite rightfully assumes value and worth. Here are lessons to be learned, traditions to be held, and customs to be cherished. Threads of family, friends, and foes embellish the failures and achievements of the colorful folk of these pages. Real people become words. It is literature, non-fiction of the heart, meticulously interwoven with rhythms and cadences that will endure as monuments to a history unique among the people of America. Metaphors and symbols may be lacking but the prose is direct, hearty, genuine, and powerful. Read, and discover a voice echoing three centuries of history on three continents. Open the past with these authors and allow them to lure you into their vision of life lived in a place and time as remote now as those of your own youth."

Dona Reeves-Marquardt, PhD, Professor Emerita,
Texas State University at San Marcos

"*Watermelons and Thistles* provides an authentic, insightful glimpse into the lives of those Germans from Russia that grew up throughout the upper Midwest. The stories and poetry included reflect a variety of locales and eras, but contain several universal themes and experiences. The North Star Chapter Germans from Russia are to be commended for not only producing a work that documents stories that are in danger of being lost, but also a volume that presents a great deal of North and South Dakota's rich history."

Robert Russell, Director of Williams Library and the
South Dakota Germans from Russia Cultural Center,
Northern State University, Aberdeen, South Dakota

WATERMELONS *and* THISTLES

Also by North Star Chapter of Minnesota:

Sei Unser Gast: A Collection of German Russian, German and Russian Recipes
Hollyhocks and Grasshoppers: Growing up German from Russia in America

WATERMELONS *and* THISTLES

Growing Up German *from* Russia *in* America

 NORTH STAR CHAPTER OF MINNESOTA *Germans from Russia*

To the members of the
North Star Chapter of Minnesota
(Germans from Russia)
in honor of our 40th anniversary year.

ISBN: 978-0-9977266-5-7

Library of Congress Control Number: 2018932252

AMBER SKYE PUBLISHING LLC

1935 BERKSHIRE DRIVE

EAGAN, MINNESOTA 55122

651-452-0463

Printed in the United States of America

Acknowledgments

Many thanks:

- to the members of the North Star Chapter of Minnesota (Germans from Russia) who shared their poems, essays, photographs and publishing funds
- to Virginia Weispfenning Peterson for providing cover art entitled "Prairie Snowfall"
- to Paul Maggitti for providing technical support
- to Jim Gessele for assistance with dialect phrases and translation

TABLE OF CONTENTS

INTRODUCTION

Book Committee at work. From left: Cindy Miller, Bernie Becker, Carol Just, Nancy Gertner, Sharon Chmielarz. (Photo courtesy of Paul Maggitti)

In the process of editing this book, Carol found in her photo collection an unidentified photo. It is iconic: a man and a woman in their garden in autumn. From their clothing we know they lived in the 50s or late 40s. That they had a small house painted white. That they're wearing go-to-town clothes but not their go-to-church clothes. We wanted so to be able to identify them. We even laughed, maybe we should include them in the book with the caption, "Do you know these people?" We have placed them on the title page.

In our own way as an editorial panel, we have edited and arranged stories that are also iconic with a German from Russia flavor. We've included names and places so they do not go lost, do not remain undiscovered, do not go looking for a home, do not remain under a bushel basket where no one else can see them. Instead readers can say, Aha! or Yes! or That's the way it was, or Did people really live like that?

We wanted these stories in a paperback book where they may feel more at home than in an e-book, though the contrast between a story of the first radio and reading about it on an i-tablet would be startling in itself!

All of the stories are at home on the prairie. All are about people who come from people who have standards for old tractors or strudel dough so thin it can be held up to the light and seen through. But not hole-y! The mouse beside your computer would be as foreign to our ancestors as a scythe would be to a twenty-first-century child.

These stories are brought from the past and laid out on this book's pages potluck-style. Each writer brings something and invites readers to partake. There's no first or last in line. Each one is a dessert, or full meal (meat and potatoes; wurst and dumplings), or a glass of water or a shot of schnapps in itself. Eat, drink the words and enjoy.

And if any reader is longing for a missing father or mother or grandparents, we have a photo just right for you.

The Editors:
Bernelda Kallenberger Becker
Sharon Grenz Chmielarz
Nancy Gertner
Carol Just
Cynthia Miller

NOTE TO READERS

What does it mean to be a German from Russia in America?

Basically it means that we descend from migrating ancestors who were German dialect speakers. Many were farmers who risked change and were willing to set down roots where they could practice their religion, keep their language, and live a peaceful agrarian life.

When the former German princess Czarina Catherine the Great, and later her grandson Czar Alexander I wanted to settle lands along the Volga River region (1763) and the region of the Black Sea (1802) they offered an enticing deal to our German ancestors who were looking for more land and peace, wanting to avoid wars that claimed taxes, crops, livestock, and worst of all, conscripted their sons to military service.

To migrate to Russia, our ancestors were expected to have skills in viniculture, livestock breeding, and have good farm and trade management skills. In addition to free land, they were allowed to keep their language, be self-governing, exercise religious freedom, and were exempt from military service. German colonists established hundreds of villages along the Volga River region and in the Black Sea area of South Russia. The first years were filled with hardship and mortality rates were high, but with hard work and perseverance, agriculture as well as business and viniculture thrived.

Once established, life was good for Germans in Russia until June, 1871, when Czar Alexander II cancelled all rights and privileges granted to the German colonists. Schools were to be "Russified," German colonies were given Russian names and were no longer self-governed. Perhaps worst of all, the sons of the colonists were required to serve in the Czar's army.

Meanwhile in America, President Abraham Lincoln signed the Homestead Act of 1862, opening vast spaces of virgin soil to homesteaders. Many of our ancestors migrated once again in search of a life with the freedoms they valued.

German colonists in Russia began leaving in significant numbers in the 1870's and migrated to North and South America, settling in Canada, the USA, Mexico, Argentina, and Brazil. Some chose to homestead in Dakota Territory, Iowa, Minnesota, Kansas, Oklahoma, and Nebraska. Others worked on the railroads in Nebraska and the sugar-beet fields in Colorado and western Nebraska. Factory jobs lured them to Sheboygan or Racine, Wisconsin, and to the Jefferson Park area of Chicago. Later, others found their way west to Washington, Oregon, and California to grow vegetables and fruits and establish vineyards. In Minnesota, Germans from Russia homesteaded farms and also worked at the St. Paul stockyards or contracted to work in the beet fields in Sibley and McLeod Counties until they had saved enough cash to buy acreage or start a business.

In 1978, Germans from Russia descendants in the Minneapolis-St. Paul area established the Minnesota North Star Chapter, Germans from Russia. For forty years, the Minnesota North Star Chapter, Germans from Russia, whose membership is made up of descendants from many different areas in the United States and Russia, has provided educational programming on the topic of the Germans from Russia. In 2013 the chapter published its first anthology *Hollyhocks and Grasshoppers: Growing Up German from Russia in America*. With this new volume, we continue to share stories of descendants, reflecting on the legacy of the Germans from Russia in America.

There is a wealth of German-language literature about the Germans from Russia but the best comprehensive English-language books are:

Bosch, William, *The German-Russians In Words and Pictures*, Spearfish, SD, 2015

Giesinger, Adam, *From Catherine to Khruschev: The Story of Russia's Germans*. Battleford, Saskatchewan, Canada, Marion Press, 1974

Height, Joseph S., *Memories of the Black Sea Germans: Highlights of their History and Heritage*, Associated German-Russian Sponsors, 1979.

Schmidt, Ute, *Bessarabia, German Colonists on the Black Sea*, Germans from Russia Heritage Collection and Deutsches Kulturforum, 2011

Stumpp, Karl, *The Emigration from Germany to Russia in the Years 1763 to 1862*. Lincoln, Nebraska: American Historical Society of Germans from Russia, 1982

You may also visit the following websites to learn more about the culture of the Germans from Russia.

http://www.northstarchapter.org/

http://library.ndsu.edu/grhc

http://cvgs.cu-portland.edu/origins.cfm

www.grhs.org

www.ahsgr.org

www.gcra.org.

www.northern.edu

FOREWORD

Prairie Memories
Bernelda Kallenberger Becker

Twenty-seven years ago, my husband, Roy, and I drove westward across the North Dakota plains on Interstate I-94. "It looks much the same," I told him. "It's been many years since I've seen the prairie of my youth." My eyes scanned the landscape, dredging up memories. Sights, once familiar, were now unfamiliar. I saw a bird flying from a broken window as we passed an abandoned farmhouse. The door hung ajar and the porch sagged. If walls could talk, I mused, what tales they could tell. In my memory, farms like these had been well kept.

The gently rolling hills and pastures were still there. Large rock piles still decorated the fields, bringing to remembrance the 1930s when our family walked alongside the horse-drawn stone boat each spring. We picked up stones that the winter's hard freeze had pushed to the soil's surface and placed them on the stone boat. When its weight became all the horses could pull, my father directed them to the closest pile of stones, where we unloaded them. Judging by the size of the piles I now saw, farmers were still picking up rocks. My husband assured me that modern equipment now made the task less arduous.

Huge fields of sunflowers dazzled us with their beauty. I could not recall this crop from my childhood. I remembered my father planting wheat and oats. "Do they harvest sunflowers with the same combine they use to harvest wheat or soybeans?" I asked. Even though we lived in a city, my Wisconsin-born husband took his hometown country paper and kept up with modern farming methods. My Dakota childhood harvest-time memories were of a horse-drawn swather, shocking bundles later threshed using a huge, noisy threshing machine that shot straw and dust into the air. Now those threshing machines, rusting and ghost-like, were displayed along the highway.

In abandoned barns the former haylofts were gaping, empty caverns no longer filled in preparation for harsh winter blizzards. My mind's eye went to a photograph in my mother's album. Sitting astride a horse-drawn hay rake my mother wore a wide-brimmed straw hat, a rayon stocking pulled over her face, holes cut in for her eyes, to prevent sunburn. Putting up hay had always been a large part of summer. But now large, round bales dotted the fields. They looked like giant white grubs in their white plastic covers.

The broken-down windmills in the deserted farmyards made me feel sad. We children used to test each other's courage to see who could climb the highest on the windmill frames. When one of the boys would reach the very top my cousin Elaine and I would screech, "You better come down or we'll tell your Mama." A crowd of transmission towers now marched across the landscape carrying electric power to every hill and vale. That power pumped the water formerly brought forth from the earth by those windmills, the sentries of the plains.

That same electric power provided an "open sesame" to modern-day conveniences. Mothers no more hung cream in the well to keep it sweet or cooled watermelons in the watering tank. Kerosene lamps were relegated to the attic. Rotary telephones replaced the party-line hand-cranked telephone since relegated to museums. Two long rings and a short were history.

One-room country schools stood along the road, paint peeling and windows boarded. My husband pointed out that the bell tower had no bell.

I noticed two outhouses behind the school, doors hanging open, swinging in the wind. We reminded each other we had used things such as the Sears catalogs and peach wrappings during canning season for toilet paper.

Driving through a town, we saw school buses lined up in the curved driveway in front of a beautiful brick school, waiting to return children to their homes across the countryside. Many of us walked a mile or two. The large athletic fields had baseball and football fields, and bleachers. We played games like pom pom pullaway, Andy-I-over, and fox and geese. There had been no playground equipment on my prairie schoolyard, not even a tree from which to hang a swing. But we had fun.

Now, another twenty-five years have passed. There have been many more changes. Ahh . . . memories. We like to be reminded of what has been. Better yet is what is now. Pictures in my mother's photo album show my grandparents dressed in their Sunday best. Stiff and solemn, never smiling. Their lives were hard. It took courage to leave all they knew in South Russia, and sail to an unknown land. They came to claim 160 acres of free land in America's unsettled Midwest. Homesteaders, they plowed the first furrows on the prairie, picked the first rocks, planted the first trees, and built the first churches and schools. Their life on the prairie made it possible for us, their offspring, to enjoy our present lives and conveniences. My albums have many photos showing people sporting happy faces and wide smiles.

Progress brings change and, in the not-too-distant future, my grandchildren will look back with nostalgia, and remember how it used to be in the early twenty-first century. When they think of the technology that had been available to us, their parents and grandparents, compared to what they will have, they'll wonder how we managed to live in such primitive circumstances, even as my husband and I wondered all those years ago as we drove Interstate I-94 westward across the North Dakota plains.

CHAPTER ONE

Iron in our Blood

Blacksmith shop, Linton, North Dakota, Ray Dockter, Proprietor.
(Photo courtesy of Carol Just)

Iron in our Blood

By Merv Rennich

During my many travels out of the country, people would ask me, "What nationality are you?" I would reply, "I am American!" Then I would add, "I was born in North Dakota, but I am first-generation American. My father was born in Russia." That would sometimes lead to a surprised look and a comment like, "But you are not Russian." Then I would further comment that my ethnicity is not Russian but rather German. That would cause another look, which would often lead to a discussion of how my ancestors on my mother's side were farmers who went from Germany to Russia in the early nineteenth century. It is not certain from where in Germany they originated, but some data indicates they came from the area of Karlsruhe in the current state of Baden-Württemberg. They ended up settling in Hoffnungstal, Bessarabia, where they lived for about sixty years before immigrating to America.

Entering Waterloo (now Stavky) from the west, 1998.

(Photo courtesy of Merv Rennich)

My father's family included blacksmiths and wagon manufacturers. They emigrated from the little village of Flinsbach, which is about twenty-five miles southeast of Heidelberg, Germany, to Waterloo (now Stavky) in the Beresan District of South Russia. They lived there for almost one hundred years before going to America in 1909 where the blacksmith trade was continued by my grandfather and father, repairing farm machinery.

As a young child, I remember hearing my grandmother lamenting about leaving Bessarabia. Once when I was in her kitchen, I recall she stopped kneading the bread dough she was preparing and, with tears in her eyes, stared out the window as she talked about how beautiful Hoffnungstal was and how she wished to be back in Bessarabia. I thought then that when I grew up I would go see that place.

When not in grade school, I would often spend time with my father in his farm implement repair shop. I would help him put machinery together by placing the washers and nuts on bolts that he would make tight using a wrench. The time spent with my father in his shop working on tractors and machinery continued into high school. With this experience and my family's blacksmith history, I decided early on that somehow I wanted to spend my future career working with "iron" like my ancestors did.

This latent desire came to fruition when I graduated from the University of North Dakota with a degree in mechanical engineering and went to work for Caterpillar Tractor Co. as an overseas/foreign field engineer working on construction machinery and diesel engines. The first fifteen years with the company were spent living in Panama and Mexico and traveling in every country in Latin America but one. Cuba came later. The nomadic trait of the family going from Germany to Russia to America continued with our oldest son being born in Mexico City.

The next five years were spent living in Switzerland from where many visits were made to Germany, some taken looking for my ancestral roots. Returning to the United States I remained connected with "iron" on a worldwide basis until my retirement. I then did more world traveling with one trip of particular note: going to Ukraine with the Germans from Russia Heritage Collection (GRHC) Journey to the Homeland Tour in 1998 led by Michael Miller.

On that trip I visited Waterloo (Stavky) and with the help of a local guide was able to talk with an elderly retired schoolmaster, Gregori Chub, who remembered my grandfather's blacksmith shop and wagon factory, telling me about it and where it was located. Somewhat ironically, it burned down during the German occupation of World War II.

The visit to my ancestral village was overwhelming. To see the houses, walk the streets, visit the cemetery, see the school that was falling into disrepair, and stand next to the church in the village where my father was born and from where my ancestors came was a very emotional experience.

The family blacksmithing legacy goes on, from the hard work of pounding hot iron, to working with machinery, to having three sons with engineering degrees.

Schoolmaster Gregori Chub, right, his wife on far left and interpreter, Galina, middle. 1998 (Photo courtesy of Merv Rennich)

Found! My Forty-Year Search for My Great-Great-Grandmother

By Carol Just

In 1974, I began my journey of discovery as I tried to create a family tree. Don't let anyone tell you it is an easy path. I was twenty-four years old and oh-so-earnest in my quest to track my family history. I soon discovered that there is no direct route. There will be dead ends and occasional road construction on the way. My goal? To go from myself backwards to as many grandparents, great-, great-great-, great-great-great-grandparents, and beyond as possible. It has been such an interesting ride. I identified many of them within the first few years and soon had their history, migration, homestead, church, birth, marriage, and death dates, and cemetery information.

The great-grandparents were easy. There were enough older relatives to interview who could give me the needed information along with great stories that blew life into the names and dates. They opened their photo albums so I could add images to my stories. Photos and stories allow you to really get to know your subject and appreciate their journey.

In the great-great-grandparent category, the path has required more complex research. Libraries, archives, ship records, census records, and citizenship, homestead, and church records all open doors and make for a different kind of experience.

Long-ago oral interviews with great-aunts and great-uncles made it clear that I descend from really interesting people. As I go back over those notes from forty years ago, I can still smell the fresh bread cooling on the cupboard. The savory dill and beet pickles they served with fresh bread, slices of thick ham, and home-churned butter—sometimes washed down with homemade wine or schnapps. Occasionally they would go out to the vine garden they called the *Bashtan* and pick a ripe melon, or go down to the cool cellar and bring up a melon that they would cut into thick slices to go

Christina Seeger Heine in sod house, circa 1890s.
(Photo courtesy of Carol Just)

with the rest of the meal. Breaking bread seemed to be the best way for them to get to know me and decide if I was someone they wanted to share their story with. Most said that they had nothing interesting to tell me, but with each sip of coffee and each bite of fruit and custard *Kuchen,* they began to talk. It was slices of heaven to listen to them speak in their accented adopted language with many German words sprinkled in. Some words and phrases simply cannot be translated.

One great-great-grandmother has eluded me since her grandson Julius Dockter told me about her in a lengthy interview in the early days of my research. Christina Seeger Heine was born in South Russia in 1830. She married Johann Heine in 1851, had nine live births, with only five surviving before she arrived at the Port of New York with her husband, Johann, and five daughters on the *SS Lessing* on November 15, 1873. We know that from there they took a train to Yankton, Dakota Territory, where they lived until arriving in McIntosh County, Dakota Territory, in 1885, where Johann, at age fifty-six, filed for a homestead claim. I have one grainy photo of Christina Seeger Heine standing in what looks like her sod house with a couple of vases of prairie grasses on the table next to her.

The fact that she raised four daughters (I'm still on the hunt for the fifth daughter) who were strong and determined makes her all the more interesting to me. I'm related to her through my great-grandmother Katharina Heine Dockter, my mother's paternal grandmother. Katharina was one of twenty-three women (out of 384 applicants) who filed homestead claims in McIntosh County, Dakota Territory, in 1886. Katharina's claim along Beaver Creek became the anchor site for that family and for generations of descendants who shared vivid memories of time spent on that farm. Her Timber Culture claim along the creek provided picnic space for the greater community long before state, county, and city parks were created as public spaces.

Christina appears with her husband, Johann, in the 1900 census as living on his homestead claim just south of her daughter Katharina's acreage. Johann Heine died in April of that year, leaving her a widow. A Declaration of Intent document following his death indicates that she decided to become a citizen—perhaps to be able to inherit and sell her husband's homestead. A later document reveals that she sold that homestead to my great-grandparents for $1,000. Her grandson Julius Dockter was only three when she died, but he knew that following Johann's death, Christina went to live with her daughter Karoline Heine Olson Heer who resided some fifty miles west in Lamoure County near the small town of Kulm, North Dakota.

When I began my search for her in 1974, no one seemed to know what happened to Christina Seeger Heine once she moved to her daughter's home, or when she died, or where she was buried. Sometime in the 1980s I stopped at the Lamoure County Court House and, after a search through the Clerk of Court records, I found a record of her death in 1909 at the age of seventy-nine.

Since Christina Seeger Heine is not buried in St Andrew's Cemetery in rural McIntosh County where her husband lies, I assumed she might be buried near her daughter Karoline Heine Olson Heer in the Kulm Congregational Cemetery. Another thing you should know is that assumptions and logic do not apply in genealogy research. I walked through that cemetery more times than I can count, and I never found a marker for her.

Fast forward to 2015. Historical society colleague and retired friend Ray Reinhardt offered to work on some of my mystery cases (all genealogists have them). I gave him what information I had about Christina Seeger Heine and he got to work. It is because of my good fortune to have such a kind friend with dogged diligence that the mystery has been solved.

Poring over microfilm of the local newspaper, the *Kulm Messenger*, Ray noticed a note of condolence to the Heer family upon the passing of Karoline Heer's mother, Christina Heine. The notice said the funeral was at St. Paul's Lutheran Church.

Aha! My silly assumption that she attended her daughter's church kept me from finding her for decades. After I finished beating myself up about it, I began to look for a cemetery attached to that church. I learned that St. Paul's had long ago closed its doors, but somewhere there had to be a cemetery.

I had hunted through the North Dakota Gravestones website for churches and cemeteries in Lamoure County, which has quite a presence on that website because of the efforts of Allen and Mary Lu Konrad. Their diligent recording of several cemeteries in Dickey, Lamoure, Logan, and McIntosh Counties is a gift to the families and to researchers. Together they have trekked from cemetery to cemetery to take photographs and upload them to the website with information about each grave. The website is a volunteer endeavor, which is why not every cemetery in every county is included. I checked for St. Paul's Cemetery in Lamoure County, since

Carol Just at Christina Heine's gravestone, July 2016.
(Photo courtesy of Carol Just)

the church's address was Kulm and Kulm is in Lamoure County. No luck! Flummoxed again!

Then late one night when I couldn't sleep I looked at the state map again and realized that Kulm, in Lamoure County, is a stone's throw (maybe one mile) north of the Dickey County line. I booted up my laptop and pulled up the North Dakota Gravestones website entering a request for Dickey County. I entered St. Paul's Lutheran Cemetery, and it popped up! Then I typed in Christine Heine, and with the click of my mouse there she appeared listing the section, township, and range in Northwest Township. Eureka! I found her! At 2 a.m., I had no one to share this so-long-in-coming discovery, but I thanked the Universe for friends like Ray Reinhardt and Allen and Mary Lu Konrad.

Now to schedule a visit to the gravesite! Arizona cousin Marge Dockter Hestermann and my brother and sister-in-law Walt and Pat Just signed on to join me. On July 19, 2016, we met in Wishek, North Dakota, and picked up our aunt Laverna Dockter Kaseman. Having no idea what shape the cemetery might be in, we borrowed tools (shovel, hedge trimmer, battery-operated grass trimmer, and gloves) and headed east to Kulm.

Let me tell you, it is not easy getting a township map. The woman at the Register of Deeds office at the Dickey County seat in Ellendale, North Dakota, said that she could not scan and email the map to me, but I could stop by and pick one up.

Unfortunately, it was many miles out of the way. My brother Walt managed to get a township map sent to me by text, but it didn't show any roads leading to the cemetery. Fortunately, Allen Konrad had an email address attached to his St. Paul Lutheran postings to the North Dakota Gravestones website. An email to him requesting directions to the cemetery resulted in this reply: "If you approach Kulm from the north, on Highway 56, continue to the south edge of town and keep on driving south for one mile. At that point the highway will make a left bend to correct for entering Dickey County. Do not drive the bend, but turn left and drive the section line road one and a half miles. You will approach some trees on the north side of the road. If you go any farther, you will meet up with a slough that has covered the once-existing road. At the trees, turn right and drive up the hill. Once on top, the cemetery is to the left." Without those directions, I might still be driving section line roads.

I can't really explain how I felt. Imagine—grave-hunting for forty years—knowing she had to be somewhere but not able to find her. As we headed to the cemetery that morning I could hardly talk. I realize it is sort of a "nerdy" endeavor, but genealogists get it. I don't know many people who can say they have been hunting for something for all those years, and when it fell into my lap, I found myself at a loss for words.

Aunt Laverna had a bouquet of flowers from her garden ready as we made our way to the cemetery. Allen Konrad's directions were completely accurate, and thankfully the cemetery was mowed and trimmed. Still, we could find no marker to match the marker Allen Konrad had placed on the North Dakota Gravestones website all those years ago. We found the area where the earliest graves were located and decided to investigate an overgrown grove of lilac bushes. My brother ventured a few feet into the lilac bushes and, aha, there she was!

We clipped away at the overgrowth, and sunlight flooded the beautiful stone that had been placed for her 107 years ago. The stone was wobbly and needed to be secured, and next to it was a large hole, probably the home of a badger. The lilac bushes had likely protected the gravestone, and maybe other stones, for years.

"I found her! I found her!" was all I could say. The cemetery in its remote location likely gets few visitors. I wondered when the last visit to her 1909 grave might have been, but I was comforted to know that Christina Seeger Heine's great-granddaughter and three of her great-great-grandchildren paid homage to her on that day.

Genealogy is part mystery, part exploration, part collaboration, and part satisfaction. On that day I could say all four parts aligned, and I felt only happiness and great satisfaction.

Previously published in GRHS Heritage Review Vol. 46, Issue 4 December 2016

Discovering Genealogy

By Merv Rennich

I would often hear my maternal grandmother exclaim, "Oh, how I wish I was back in Hoffnungstal!" She and her parents and also my father and his parents came to America from Bessarabia and the Beresan District of South Russia just after the turn of the twentieth century. They were tested by the hard life of homesteading on the central North Dakota prairie. But on Sundays and holidays we gathered together, grandparents, parents, aunts, uncles, and cousins. We children listened to the elders talk about family and life in the "old country" because as youngsters we were to be seen and not heard.

Many of their stories stuck with me, and my interest in them was rekindled when I received a copy of Karl Stumpp's 1,018-page book titled *The Emigration from Germany to Russia in the Years 1763 to 1862* while I was living in Geneva, Switzerland, in 1976. Paging through the thick volume for several hours, I finally found a three-line entry of my family name on page 804 under the general heading Waterloo.

> *Rennich, Jakob 61, seine Frau Christine 56, seine*
> *Kinder Martin 25, Jakob 22, Georg 19, Anton 12,*
> *Margareta + 1833. (Von Kol.Friedrichsthal Nr. 42.)*

I then recalled my father mentioning Waterloo as the place where he was born–Waterloo, South Russia, founded in 1819 by immigrants from Germany and named after Waterloo, a Belgian village whose inhabitants refused to give up during the battle where Napoleon was finally defeated in 1815. It was the first documented piece of evidence I had of the family's connection to the "old country" as my grandparents referred to it. And on top of that I had the name of where they came from in Germany: Friedrichstal. What a discovery! I would find this Friedrichstal and learn a lot more about my ancestry.

Published family history books. (Photo courtesy of Merv Rennich)

Since my family and I were living in Geneva, I scoured a German road map and found a town by the name of Friedrichstal a few miles north of Karlsruhe, Germany. This must be where my ancestors came from.

My wife wanted to take the children to the zoo in Basel, Switzerland, which is located on the Rhine River on the border with Germany about 120 miles south of Karlsruhe. After dropping them off, I motored on to Friedrichstal. It was a small village and I soon found the cemetery. I started to methodically check the gravestones for the family name, but could not find a single one with our name even after I checked them all again. How discouraging that was. Neither the town's church nor library was any help. So much for genealogy research, I thought.

After we moved back to the United States I attended a Germans from Russia Heritage Society (GRHS) convention in Bismarck, North Dakota. There I met and discussed Friedrichstal with my cousin Dale Wahl, and learned that Stumpp's book referred to a settlement colony in South Russia, not in Germany. It was abandoned; many of the residents had resettled in Waterloo. That answered a few questions I had and created others.

Further discussions with Dale rekindled my interest in family research, which led to a number of adventures. With Dale, I attended the Bessarabian *Bundestreffen* in Germany and met many unknown cousins who survived the war. I also traveled with Michael Miller of the Germans from Russia Heritage Collection at North Dakota State University to Ukraine where I visited both my paternal and maternal ancestral villages of Waterloo, Beresan District, and Hoffnungstal, Bessarabia. Back home, I edited the *Beresan Newsletter* for a few years, and, with my cousin DarEl Weist, wrote a 200-page genealogy book of my maternal ancestors, the Kleingartners. I also wrote a Rennich genealogy book for which my grandson Nathan created the cover. I have almost 5,000 names in my Family Tree Maker database. One branch of the tree goes as far back as 1550.

I continued attending a number of Germans from Russia Heritage Society conventions and became a member of the North Star Chapter of Minnesota. I also gave talks on blacksmithing, my grandfather's occupation, and on growing up in central North Dakota.

For almost four decades we searched for the place in Germany my ancestors came from. Finally the Rennich mystery was solved. My cousin Betty Rennich hired a genealogy researcher in Salt Lake City who found in GSFilm Number 1882641; Digital Folder Number 004280439-a record of my third great-grandfather Jacob Rennich born in Flinsbach, Germany, on December 19, 1774 (Flinsbach is located about twenty-five miles southeast of Heidelberg). Several more generations were added onto to the family tree We were elated!

The joy of genealogy not only comes from making a new discovery, of searching until a new piece of family data is uncovered, but of also passing this on to my children and the rest of the family.

CHAPTER TWO

Tales from the SauerkrautTriangle

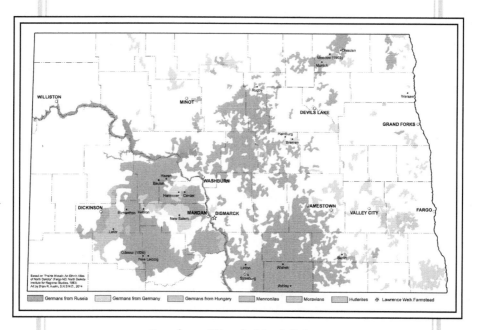

Sauerkraut Triangle, North Dakota
(Photo courtesy of State Historical Society of North Dakota)

Are You German?

By William (Bill) Bosch

My hearing is poor. It has been evaluated by two different offices that sell hearing aids, and they said that I probably would not benefit from a hearing aid. Bummer. I am tempted to try one of those thirty-day return options. I miss a lot of conversations due to bad ears.

In September 2016, Allen Kleinsasser gave the keynote address at our national convention of the Germans from Russia Heritage Society. His voice and my ears mesh beautifully and I heard every word he spoke. He told of his experiences working for the Rapid City Water Department. During his time, Rapid City installed new water meters throughout the city. One resident was a woman who was very shy or suspicious of strangers and no one had been able to get access to her house or yard to install a new meter. So with a round of chuckles in the warehouse, they dispatched Allen to her residence. I may have a few details wrong but the general thrust of his story is as follows.

When he rang her doorbell, she opened the door a few inches and asked, "Who are you?"

"I'm from the Water Department and I'm here to put in a new water meter for you."

"How do I know you're not some kind of crook or robber?"

"Well, Ma'am, it says right here on my shirt, 'Rapid City Water Department.'"

"You could have taken that off someone's wash line."

"Well, Ma'am, if you look out in the street, my van is parked out there and on its side it says 'Rapid City Water Department.'"

"You could have stolen that, too."

At that point she had opened the door a few more inches and Allen saw something hanging on the wall with some German words on it. Allen either remarked about the words or recited some of them to which she replied, "Are you German?"

"Yes, Ma'am, I am German."

She swung the door wide open and said, "Come on in."

A little while later she had a new meter and Allen was sitting at her kitchen table enjoying some conversation and coffee. Knowing Allen, he probably left with a fresh loaf of banana bread under his arm. His buddies back at the warehouse awaited his return with much anticipation.

"So, Allen, how did it go?" they asked with smirks on their faces.

"No problem at all. I installed a new meter and that was that," replied Allen nonchalantly. They are probably still scratching their heads down there over that incident. Sometimes it is an advantage to be a "German" and sometimes it isn't.

About a month after that convention, I was in Linton, North Dakota. My brother and I had taken on a small construction project. Our great-grandfather Gottlieb Dockter is buried in a rural cemetery north of Zeeland, North Dakota. It is called Frieden's Lutheran Cemetery. He has an iron cross over his grave. He wife, Salomea, is buried right beside but has nothing over her grave. Gottlieb and Salomea emigrated from Neudorf, South Russia, to Dakota Territory in 1889. My second cousin once removed Carol Just, who lives in Minnesota, had talked to me about putting a cross over her grave. After a couple of years of hesitation, we finally agreed to move on that project.

My brother and I volunteered to put up a base for an iron cross. Our cousin, who is also a great-grandson of Salomea, volunteered to build a cross for her. His name is Ray Dockter and he lives in Linton, North Dakota, where he still works as a blacksmith at about eighty years of age.

So sometime in October 2016 my white Toyota truck was parked in front of my brother's house and we were loading supplies to make the trip to the cemetery and sink a concrete pillar into the ground for a base for the cross. My brother had gone to the rear of his house while I was still loading.

Bill Bosch with his white truck. (Photo courtesy of Bill Bosch)

The door on the house next door opened a bit and a woman poked out her head and asked, "Could you fix my faucet?"

To say I am not good at repairing faucets is an understatement. In fact, whenever I undertake a plumbing job in our house it is likely to turn into an event worthy of being included in our annual Christmas letter. But I did not want to be unfriendly. For all I knew maybe her faucet was spraying water up to the ceiling and she needed help right then and there. So I said, "Well, I suppose I could take a look at it."

She asked, "Are you German?"

Aha, she was appealing to my ethnic pride. Clever woman. With Allen's successful approach still firmly in mind, I squared up my shoulders and stuck my chest out a bit and replied, "Yes, I am German."

"No, you're not."

"Ma'am, I most certainly am German."

"No, you're not."

"Yes, I am. I assure you that I am German."

"No, you're not. There can't be two of you."

"Two of us? There are hundreds of us. This town is full of Germans and I am one of them."

"No, you're not," she said and closed her door.

Oh, well. I had other things to do and she could do what she wanted. I continued loading supplies for our construction project. The conversation puzzled me, though, and I wondered about it until someone familiar with the community explained it to me.

Linton, North Dakota, is a town of about 1,400. They have one plumber. His white truck looks a lot like my truck. And his name is Sherman.

Previously published in the *Black Hills Chapter Newsletter,*
Volume 22, Issue 1, February 2017.

Prairie Fire!

David Delzer

Prairie fires were a big concern in the early years for our ancestors. Homesteaders were required to cultivate forty acres to prove up their quarter section. They also were required to live on the land they were proving up. Proving up took five years, and breaking ten acres was considered a good year. Our German from Russia ancestors would settle down on their homestead and either build a sod house or put together a shack with whatever lumber they could haul on a wagon. The homesteaders would use their plows to provide a black dirt barrier, or fire break, around their living space and hope that it would divert any flames that might come roaring across the prairie. A prairie fire south of Belfield, North Dakota, claimed the lives of several school children and their teacher in 1914. They evacuated their schoolhouse when they saw smoke and almost made it to a field that had been plowed. Prairie fires are mentioned at least a dozen times in oral histories of early settlers in McLean County, North Dakota.

Our family farm in northern McLean County was just east of a range of hills left by a glacier. The tallest of these hills was noted by the French explorer Verendrye in his 1738 exploration of the western Dakotas. It was named Blue Hill. It is visible four miles from the east, where our farm is, and for at least ten miles. The hills form the east edge of Township 150 N, Range 85 W, a township named appropriately Blue Hill. Early settlers did their best to prove up their homesteads there but much of the hilly, rocky land left by the glacier soon reverted to pasture land. Some of it still remains native prairie and has never been broken.

In the 1940s a large prairie fire broke out in those hills. Farmers from our area (just to the east of Blue Hill Township) rushed to fight it. My father and my uncles Joyce and Randall were among the neighbors who hurried to fight the fire. The fire was eventually stopped about one mile west of our farm and really close to the farms of some of our neighbors. It was stopped by farmers who created a firebreak with their tractors and plows. I think the wind must have shifted and the farmers were able to extinguish residual flames by beating them with wet gunnysacks and digging with pitchforks, shovels, and spades. One of my uncles got so excited he forgot to bring his plow. There were at least three farms directly in the path of the fire that were no doubt saved by the quick action of those who responded.

Patrolling the burnt area on his tractor, my father drove across a quarter section of land that he later bought and used as pasture. The burnt prairie revealed two different areas where Native Americans had set up camp using rocks the glacier left to anchor the poles of their tepees and to build fire rings. These Indian campsites were used in summer by hunting parties and were located close to sloughs—shallow sources of water on the prairie. The campsites were located where they could look across the plains to the east for herds of buffalo. These Indian rings can still be located but with difficulty as the grass has grown up around them. The Indians' winter homes were by the Missouri River but they hunted and foraged on the prairie in summer.

The Farmall Super M tractor was one of the most-widely produced of International Harvester's "letter series" tractors. Equipped with a four-cylinder engine, a six-volt electrical system, and a transmission with six gears, the standard M's purchase price in 1952 was $2,400.

My personal experience with prairie fires involved two occurrences, both during harvest time. In the fall of my senior year in high school my grandfather and I were combining barley on our two west quarters. Dad had broken up the east quarter and divided it into twenty-acre strips alternating wheat, barley, and summer fallowing. The west quarter, just on the edge of the next township and well into the hills, had three strips broken. The rest of the quarter, approximately one hundred acres, was native prairie and had never been broken. Grandpa Oran and I had our combine and tractor, a swather, and my uncle Joyce's combine and truck. Uncle Joyce had been working with us but was working summer fallow on his land nearby. Dad was hauling cattle and I stayed out of school to harvest. It was getting late in the fall and we needed to get the crop in. Grandpa had picked me up in his 1950 red International pickup and we were going to work.

We were setting up to get started on the west edge of the east quarter when Grandpa pointed to a grey cloud just to the west of us. "That looks like a prairie fire; we had better move our machinery onto the summer fallow," he said. So I pulled the Super M and the new combine onto the black dirt, hopped into my uncle's grain truck, and under Grandpa's direction backed up to my uncle's John Deere combine. I heard a clunk and a holler. "Pull ahead and back up SLOW," Grandpa said. I did and Grandpa secured the combine with a log chain. We pulled it over to the summer fallow field, disconnected it, and did the same with the swather.

Uncle Joyce showed up with his tractor and a disc plow and plowed a fire break from the summer fallow across the barley field, past a rock pile, and through some of the prairie to a summer fallow field on the west quarter. Grandpa and I hopped into the pickup and headed through the north summer fallow field toward the fire. We wanted to see just what was going on. We got near the west end of the field down in a little dip and I killed the engine. We looked up and saw the prairie in flames fifteen feet high maybe one hundred feet ahead of us. WOW!

The Douglas Volunteer Fire Department showed up shortly afterward. The prairie fire had stopped at the edge of the summer fallow fields and at my uncle's hurriedly plowed fire furrows. We welcomed the Fire Department as they were able to stop any backwards migration of the fire and to extinguish any smoldering embers. My mother had seen the smoke from our home almost four miles away. She was glad to find out we were all okay.

Back in school our English teacher expounded on the prairie fire incident. I could only hide my face in embarrassment and proclaim, "Oh, it wasn't as bad as all that. We didn't lose any combines or anything like that." I could have said, "The fire was mostly on our land and only harmed thirty or forty acres. It was good it got stopped."

The second occurrence was almost a year later and less spectacular, no doubt due to the location and the quick response of residents. I was custom combining for a neighbor who Dad often trucked cattle for. His farm was just on the west side of the string of hills. I pulled the combine out there and was getting started when I noticed a fire in the pasture just east of where I was, near a farmstead. I saw the farm lady go out to fight the fire and I went to help her. Pretty soon a whole bunch of neighbors showed up and we beat the fire out with wet burlap bags. It was good we got there quickly.

Prairie fires were an integral part of the dynamics of the prairie. Between the massive buffalo herds and the periodic burning of prairie grass, brush and timber never got a chance to take hold. A large herd of buffalo would graze a portion of the prairie down as far as they could reach. Any bushes or small trees would be used as back rubs to rid the animals of insect pests and would just plain be pushed over. Prairie fires started by lightning or by Indians, either by accident or on purpose. The tribe might start a fire to help herd the buffalo to where they could hunt them. Their method of cooking using campfires was vulnerable to a sudden gust of wind or to carelessness. As homesteaders worked to own their piece of land it took them some time to cultivate much of it. So whenever prairie fires started they were a very real menace to our early settlers. The prairie fire episodes I've described were examples of events that our German from Russia ancestors and other settlers were threatened with and which they were fortunate to have survived.

Storms of the Century:
The Blizzards of 1949, 1950, and 1951
David Delzer

My wife, Linda, and I recently watched a public television program documenting a series of blizzards that hammered the northern and western plains from January to April 1949. It highlighted the storms' effects, mostly in Wyoming, but throughout the entire region of the plains. It enumerated the repercussions of the blizzards and unselfish sacrifice, generosity, hope, and heroism of the plains dwellers who were snowed in.

My recollections of the blizzards of '49 are that of a young school child just learning to read and write in a country school. My first school term was for eight months from Labor Day 1948 until the end of April 1949. We had a lot of snow that winter. My memories of that winter and the ones that followed were of being snowed in for weeks at a time, not being able to travel very far. Snow would drift up across the roads and around buildings. A large drift would form between our house and the barn. Dad had a herd of registered Herefords and four milk cows. He had a new barn and an existing one that was used to shelter livestock. Dad had invested in a hay baler, a 50T International, that he used to bale hay for our cows and that he hired out to bale for neighbors. The first winter I was in school was before the Rural Electric Association had provided us with electricity. We were requested to hang a lantern from poles already in so snow removal crews would know where our farms were.

Our yellow farmhouse was essentially three buildings joined together, heated with a kerosene stove. We had our own source of electricity, a generator that provided us some lighting and power in the house and also the barn. One

Julius Just on top of garage after major North Dakota blizzard, circa 1941.
(Photo courtesy of Carol Just)

evening while Dad was doing chores, Mom decided to do some ironing with her new electric iron. Out went the lights! "Oh my, I'm in trouble now!" she exclaimed. Dad came in, checked the generator, and restarted it. They decided that the ironing would have to wait until daylight.

The storms in January snowed us in. The county's snow removal equipment was inadequate and we had to make do until March or April. Dad walked to town to get some of the things we needed. He pulled a sled and actually walked over the top of a neighbor's car north of us that had been drifted over. The Burgeson children were driven to just west of the schoolhouse and left there because a giant drift had formed over the road just south of the school. It was a happy day when we saw a tracked vehicle called a Weasel coming up the road from the south. We had heard that the National Guard with their snow removal equipment would be right behind it.

When the road got plowed out in the spring, some of us school children got in trouble for standing on top of the plowed drifts and throwing snowballs at the Burgesons' car. We boys had to climb over a pretty good drift to make it to the boys' outhouse. We were not allowed to leave "yellow snow" outside the school. When the snow melted, a small lake formed just to the west of the schoolyard temporarily until the ice in the culvert melted. Then the runoff traversed naturally from Dad's land, underneath the road to Uncle Joyce's and then on down through the Wollmuths' land to Douglas Creek. We had our school picnic and our fathers went to work doing the spring seeding.

In my second year of school, the winter again brought a lot of snow and many people couldn't travel. Our teacher, Mary Ellen Blonigan, drove from Douglas, but when the roads got bad, she boarded with the Wollmuth family. The two Burgeson boys spent the winter in California with family. One blizzardy day it was blowing and snowing so hard we couldn't see to walk home. My schoolmate Loretta Wollmuth's dad, Melvin, came for us. The Wollmuths lived across the road from us, between our farm and the school. Mr. Wollmuth tied Loretta, Miss Blonigan, and me to a rope and guided us back to their house. I stayed there overnight until the storm subsided. The school was cold and drafty so our teacher set her chair down on the middle of the furnace register and seated three of us younger children together. That's how we stayed warm and went to school during the winter months.

Spring came but there was a snowstorm on April 30, the day our school picnic was scheduled. Dad loaded Mom, my three sisters, and I into the '34 Ford and we headed to the school house and the picnic. When Dad got to the intersection he decided to take a shortcut. He jumped the ditch and headed directly up the rise to the schoolhouse. We hopped out of the car, took our treats inside, and enjoyed an indoor picnic. When it was time to go home the other men helped Dad shovel out and we left by the school driveway.

The M29 Weasel was a World War II vehicle, built by Studebaker, designed with tracks for operation in snow. After the war, many of the surplus vehicles were sold to allied countries.

When I was in third grade, a new first-grader, Marilyn Miller, joined our school and her dad had an airplane. When the roads got blocked up with snow he would fly Marilyn to school. He would land on my dad's field just north of the school, drop Marilyn off, and fly into Douglas, bringing back mail and groceries for the neighbors. Our new teacher, Mr. Polishuck, drove a big maroon car that got him to our school from his home north of Douglas on the road to Minot. It was a good car but not a snowplow so when the roads got blocked he stayed close. I remember going with him to help shovel and clear the roads east of our place. We worked hard and got maybe a mile and a half before we turned back.

I helped my dad load up bales of hay to haul across the river to ranchers that were in need. We knew about the troubles getting food to herds of cows out there. Our livestock and that of our neighbors were generally somewhat sheltered against the harsh winters. The herds of cattle further west where winters were generally not as severe were not so sheltered. The work of the Civil Air Patrol and others was indeed needed to keep them from starving.

The TV special we saw concentrated on the 1949 blizzards and their effect in the area of eastern Wyoming. Those of us on the plains of North Dakota had similar experiences, and not just in 1949. Now improved roadways and modern snow removal equipment have helped immeasurably. Roads may be closed for a short while but are soon opened thanks to these improvements. It is good it is so.

Uphill Both Ways

Cynthia Miller

"In winter we always had to walk to school through six feet of snow!" my dad would say.

"Uphill both ways!" an uncle would add.

"Barefoot!" a great-uncle would shout, and the adults would dissolve into hearty laughter. We kids would grimace, not just because the joke wasn't funny the tenth time around, but because the basic facts of the story were still true for us. I don't remember my parents ever driving us to school, and buses were only for the country kids. True, we only lived four blocks from school but in western North Dakota, winter could last from November to April, and that was a lot of wind and snow to clomp through.

Our mothers saw that we were dressed properly. Many kids wore full snowmobile suits every day; for the rest of us, snow pants would do. I once had a hood trimmed in real fur, outgrown by one of my cousins who lived in Alaska. Scarves went over our noses and mouths and tied behind our necks. Snow boots came up to our knees. I feel fortunate now that I started school in the '70s, when it was acceptable for girls to wear pants.

I also can now appreciate the incredible helpfulness of snow blowers. My mother and her younger sisters grew up next door to their cousin Kelly, who was an only child and like a big brother to them. They had to walk across the railroad yard to get to school, and it was Kelly's job to walk first and break a path for the younger girls after a snowstorm. For families who didn't have a tall, strapping boy, the mothers went out, bundled in headscarves, to make a trail that would hopefully last until the next big snowfall. My mother's route came out at the back of one of the bars on Main Street, and the owners would often let the children walk through the bar to have a few minutes of warmth.

We walked on sidewalks that had been cleared by our dads, snowbanks on either side of us often up to our waists. These snowbanks were valuable to us. There was nothing better to make proper caves and tunnels, if someone could figure out how to do it without them collapsing and hide them well enough from other kids who would try to take over the space. My house was at the bottom of a small hill, and one side of the front yard was a scoria-rock wall built into the earth by my dad. This was helpful for only having to make three walls to have a snow fort, which my dad would spray with water so it would freeze and last longer.

I live in Minnesota now, described as the State of Hockey. But hockey wasn't as big of a deal in western North Dakota decades ago, perhaps because of the lack of lakes and indoor ice arenas. My city would flood a large section of ground and bank up two feet of snow around it. There were no Zambonis so it got as rough and pocked as any lake ice would have. It helped to wear two pairs of underwear for when you fell on your bottom. My friend Kristy lived on a farm, and her dad would flood a small depression near her house under the yard light so we could skate at night, then run inside to put our freezing feet in warm water.

Everyone had a sled, but sliding down snow-packed hills on large pieces of cardboard was fun as well. I only had to walk across the street to find the perfect hill, which meant after a few hours of sledding, it took just minutes to get home and wrap up in a blanket with a cup of hot chocolate. All the kids had a favorite place to sled because my hometown was on a series of hills, from a small river valley north to glacier-carved ridges near Lake Sakakawea. I'm still stunned to see what passes for an "ice house" in Minnesota these days: large-screen plasma TVs with satellite cable, cozy beds, nearly-full kitchens, plowed streets, pizza delivery. An ice house on Sakakawea in the '70s was a small plywood hut with holes in the ice cut in each corner and a stool or lawn chair to sit on, with a space heater if you were lucky. Still, we enjoyed going out to the lake in the winter. I was never a fisher, but it was great for skating, snowmobiling, and sledding. I'll never forget the thrill of sledding down a large hill and sliding across the frozen lake for what felt like a mile.

We had indoor responsibilities, particularly in December. Practice for the Christmas Eve Sunday School program at my Lutheran church was held every Saturday from Thanksgiving to Christmas, and it seemed like it took all morning long. We could take off our coats but our feet sweat in our snow boots. The church was crowded with children from preschool through high school freshmen; you weren't relieved of program duty until you were confirmed. We were given our Bible verse – or "piece" – to memorize at the first practice. When I was young, the little kids had to be angels and shepherds, and the older kids got to be Mary and Joseph. I looked forward to being older and someday getting to play Mary. But when I got older, it was decided that the program was much cuter with the smaller children playing all the parts. So I never did get to be Mary. But the sting was lessened by getting our sacks at the end of the night, after walking out of church singing "Stille Nacht" for the old folks even though we couldn't speak German. The paper bags were filled with peanuts, an apple or orange (not as exciting to 1970s kids), boxes of Cracker Jack, LifeSavers, a pack of Wrigley's gum (I always hoped for Juicy Fruit), and chocolate.

But after Christmas, the winter was still very long. When I got older, I picked up cross-country skiing, gliding around the baseball diamond next to my house. We were not as interested in going outside for recess at school, which was almost never held indoors on account of weather. On the coldest days in sixth grade, some of us girls would purposely commit a slight infraction – talking too loudly in the bathrooms or passing a note – so we would have noon recess taken away as punishment. I don't know if the teachers realized that it wasn't a punishment to sit quietly at my desk reading or writing a story, warm and toasty, while my classmates bundled up to huddle around the playground and pass the time warning the younger students not to stick their tongues on the metal play set.

In high school I was a cheerleader for the wrestling team, which meant spending winter Saturday mornings on a bus for two or three hours

Cynthia Miller and her snow sled after a major snowfall, circa 1972.
(Photo courtesy of Cynthia Miller)

to make an eight o'clock weigh-in for a tournament. One bitterly cold night, with the temperature at least twenty below, I left the house in the brittle darkness to walk to school for the bus. My mother heard me go down the stairs and got up to tell me that this once she would give me a ride. But in the few minutes it took for her to get to the door to call to me, I was already a block up the hill. The cheerleaders had to sit in the front of the bus near the coaches, and on one trip there was a window that had a chunk of glass missing. There was no choice but to sit in the seat next to it, one of my fellow cheerleaders and I wrapped in a sleeping bag, huddled together, only our eyes peeking out from scarves and hats, listening to the whistle of the winter air as the bus sped down the frozen highway.

It seemed we had more interesting things to do than my father and his friends did twenty-five years previously. My dad said that when they got bored in the winter, the guy who had the toughest vehicle would let them all pile in and they found a gravel road on the edge of town that hadn't been plowed. The driver would slam the car into the snowdrifts until it was stuck, then they would all get out to shovel it free. They would crowd back in and give it another go, until they got tired of it. It seemed to me to be a game one would tire of extremely quickly.

One thing we learned from our parents was to not leave town from November to May in a car without a winter survival kit. Someone probably profited from creating an official one to sell but we made our own: a bag of extra hats, gloves, scarves, and socks; an old sleeping bag; a candle and matches for heat and light; an empty coffee can to melt snow to drink or use as a bathroom (I never thought much about what would happen if you confused the two); a bag of high-energy snacks like peanuts, M&Ms, a Hershey's chocolate bar, granola bars. I can truthfully say I never got myself into a situation where I needed my winter survival kit. I would dig it out of the trunk in June and treat myself to slightly stale snacks. Jumper cables were also a must, along with a small shovel, and a window scraper. There was no excuse for not being prepared to travel through a North Dakota winter.

There was, however, a crystal purity to the winter air that I didn't fail to appreciate for at least a few seconds every time I went outside, until the abject cold hit me, and my mind and body grumbled to themselves for the thousandth time, asking if it was ever going to get warmer. When my son was younger, he used to open his mouth to the frozen sky and say he was "drinking air." Although I know better than to take too deep of a breath when it's below zero, I try to be grateful for air so sparkling and clear.

Spring always seemed to arrive slowly. I've always been drawn to the line in the carol "In the Bleak Midwinter" that says, "Snow had fallen ... snow on snow." The song is referring to December, but to me it made more sense in reference to February or March. Some years we were lucky to get a "January thaw"–perhaps the temperature would reach forty degrees for a day or two, melting a few inches off the snow piles. Then we could be in for another two or three months of winter. As kids we didn't mind so much but it got less fun as we got older. I didn't want to wear boots to ruin my outfits in high school and didn't want to wear a hat to squash my carefully styled hair. There were many springs where a new Easter dress was worn under a winter coat.

But by April we could be assured we would start to see puddles and bare spots on the ground around the trunks of trees. Ice chunks and large branches would float swiftly by on the Knife River. You could often feel the wind shifting from north to south. The dark crusts of snow at the curbs folded inward and then ran in the gutters. There would be a day when you could take your coat off when you walked home from school. Our moms talked about "spring cleaning." Gardeners looked through seed catalogs. Snowplows and shovels were put in the back of sheds, and hoes, hoses, and watering cans brought to the front.

I was a town kid so the seasons didn't make or break my family's livelihood like it did for my farm friends. But the expectation and appreciation for four distinct and different seasons is bone deep. Winters spent in London and Phoenix, while exciting and unusual for me, gave me a gnawing sense that something was wrong. My world was not supposed to have green bushes without snow in December. It seems now there are many more too-warm winters than I remember, even sometimes rain on Christmas Day. It bothers me for a lot of reasons, but a big one is that my mind still has a reel it plays in winter where streetlights are causing a million twinkles on fresh snow, the sky is clear and dark with an ice cream moon, and while you can see the wind shaking the evergreens, you can't hear it in the trees because there are no leaves. Just an invisible stream of ice whistling past your face telling you to get inside soon, get warm, find light, because spring is still a long ways off.

Foot in Mouth: A Politician Speaks

James Gessele

From earliest settler days, Brush Lake—a jewel of a lake two miles north of my hometown, Mercer, North Dakota—was a favorite stop for politicians on the hustings because of its ability to attract crowds. Beginning with June primary elections, candidates faced the challenge of maximizing their exposure to a North Dakota electorate sparse in number and scattered wide. Brush Lake was the lure that brought people together. My own great-grandfather, Wilhelm Wagner, was wise enough to see this when he ran for representative in the state legislature in 1928 and pressed the flesh at the lake. He won that election and ostensibly represented his entire constituency, even though he spoke German almost exclusively and broken English at best.

The lake's early flirtation with politics came in 1915 when the Brush Lake Union took charge of the July 4 celebration. The Union, likely influenced by the once Dakota Farmers' Alliance and now an offshoot of A. C. Townley's newly organized Non-Partisan League, was a tight, disciplined group of Wise Township farmers. Apparently, the move to take charge of the lake event where the Commercial Club left off raised no hackles. The Union reportedly performed very well.

In 1926, before the townsmen even had time to organize a 1926 event calendar, the Women's Federated Non-Partisan Clubs of McLean County had leased the lakeside facilities for their sixth annual picnic on June 25. Foremost, it was a political gathering, but, all the same, the day started off with a baseball game between Mercer and Washburn. A crowd of more than 1,000 people appeared that day (arriving in over 200 autos) to hear lots of speeches and old-time politicking, interspersed with band music from twelve Crooked Lake farm boys. North Dakota senator Lynn Frazier gave the major address of the day. The infamous William Langer had been invited to speak but was unable to attend. At that time, speaking engagements before Non-Partisan League gatherings were his bid to erase the grief he had caused the party during his tenure as Attorney General from 1916 to 1920, to atone for the smear tactics he had used against party candidates in the 1920 election, and to resurrect a flagging political career. Langer would truly make his mark at Brush Lake with a future appearance.

Having done sufficient League penance, Langer went on to win the governorship in 1932 on the Non-Partisan ticket. By spring 1934 he was facing federal fraud charges and was convicted by a federal court jury on June 17. In spite of his conviction, he vowed to run in the upcoming primary election and went on the road defending himself, at the same time soliciting funds for his legal defense. On June 19, he appeared at a joint McLean and Sheridan Counties Non-Partisan League rally at Brush Lake. Wherever he appeared, crowds remained hushed as he made an entrance and then the throng broke out in a tumultuous, foot-stomping, hand-clapping welcome. His reception at Brush Lake was no different.

Mounting the outdoor bandstand, Langer immediately waded into a vilifying harangue of his political enemies, and of the trial judge and of the trial jury that had convicted him two days earlier. Of the twelve jurors, he reserved special comment about those of Norwegian descent when he charged—to quote a newspaper account—"they were the most stupid people, and those that had remained behind in Norway were not quite as stupid as those who had emigrated."

Langer's bitter words were met with utter, prolonged silence from otherwise rabid supporters, for he had just blasphemed Mercer's star baseball player and the town's most upstanding businessman, Ole S. Hjelle, son of Norwegian immigrants and a member of the jury that had convicted the maverick politician.

The only record of this episode is found in an old man's letter to a German-language newspaper and in the recollection etched in the mind of a man who, as a fourteen-year-old lad, witnessed a mortifying moment in politics. Were it not for German from Russia Wilhelm Goll of Martin, North Dakota, and his letter in the October 12, 1934, *Dakota Freie Presse* or the vivid recollection of Lee Lierboe, who passed away in 2009 in Eden Prairie, Minnesota, we would not know of the rare moment "Wild Bill" Langer stuck his foot in his mouth.

Previously published in *The History of Brush Lake: From Ice Age to a Summer Resort*, 2007

A Boy, His Wheels, and The Inspector
Charles Kurle

Some memories fade as time rolls on, especially the early childhood memories. Others remain almost as vivid as the day they happened. Case in point: When I was four or five, my two older brothers graduated to bicycles. Their somewhat scuffed and scratched red and chrome tricycle was now all mine!

My dad, Ray Kurle, told me to stay in the yard and not to ride my tricycle to "the shop," the implement and lumber business that he and my uncles Alvin and Morris owned in Bowdle, South Dakota. I really liked going there because it was always busy and most of the people were Germans from Russia. They used some German words in their many conversations. J. Kurle & Sons was started in 1912 by my grandfather Jacob. He was the first Kurle, along with his sister Eva, to emigrate from Russia through Ellis Island, arriving on May 9, 1895.

Maybe it was a feeling of independence or the warm summer breeze, but one day while pedaling my very own trike I had the impulse to ride farther than our yard. I remembered my dad's admonition, but that didn't seem to matter. I triked through the gravel alley, then along Main Street, passing the Bowdle Creamery and the Bell Telephone building. Half a block more and I parked in front of the huge glass windows and walked in, beaming with pride at having pedaled there all by myself. My dad would be so proud of me. Or so I thought.

His stern look told me he knew how I got there. He asked the question I could not answer. I suspect my mom used the telephone to notify my dad of my excursion. Dad had to walk around from behind the parts counter giving me a couple seconds. I whipped around, ran out, hopped on my trusty tricycle, and started pedaling home. "Someone" was right behind me moving just as fast as I could pedal. *Wup* went his hand on my rear end. That was all the inspiration I needed to push my little legs even faster. I could hear the pounding of his footsteps. My heart was pounding. I didn't want to get paddled again. I peddled furiously. I don't know when Dad stopped chasing me. When I arrived home he was nowhere to be seen. The rest of that day remains a blur. But I never again rode my tricycle to Dad's business.

A few years later, and much wiser at following "the rules," I was allowed to pedal my shiny new red and white two-wheel bicycle to my dad's business. Doing chores like washing dishes, vacuuming, cutting the grass, and cutting dough for *Knoepfla* and sauerkraut are not the most exciting childhood memories. But riding my brand new, not "hand-me-down" two-wheel bicycle is the kind of memory that pops into mind.

Learning to ride was a quick lesson. In the alley behind our house I climbed on my bike while my dad held it upright. "Turn in the direction you are tipping," was all the instruction he gave. As he helped me balance, I started to pedal. "Turn in the direction you are tipping" he repeated as he let go of my bike. About ten feet later I was on the ground. "Try again, and don't forget to turn in the direction you are tipping," he said as I hopped on for another try.

"Don't let go," I said as I rolled along. "OK," my dad said. A few seconds later I was feeling confident and said, "You can let go now." I heard him call, "I already did." Wow, I was riding on my own!

After a few days of practice, I was allowed to venture around town with friends as long as I first let my mom know where I was going. And more than once, Dad would call home just to make sure I was following the rules.

I enjoyed riding my bike to "the shop." When you walked in the door, on your left, shiny white washing machines and electric clothes dryers greeted you. Then you passed shelves of paint and paint brushes, two offices, the parts counter for farm machinery parts, and a little farther down the aisle, the door to the repair shop. It usually had at least one or more tractors in

Jacob K. Kurle and son Ray Kurle, circa 1939.
(Photo courtesy of Chuck Kurle)

various stages of repair. It also had metal working machines like a large lathe, a milling machine, large pedestal grinder, a welding machine, and a silage cutter knife sharpener. What a great place to explore.

Trips to the shop were almost always fun, except when that old gentleman they called the "sewer and water inspector" was around. He was an old farmer who retired in town. An average-sized man, a little on the heavy side, he had a somewhat wrinkled face that you would expect from enduring hot summers and cold, blizzardy Dakota winters back in the 1950s. He was always snooping around. In his heavy German accent, he'd ask questions, sometimes so many that people would stop talking or tell him they didn't know and just walk away. I guess that is why they called him "The Inspector." I always avoided getting too close to him because I didn't want him to ask me any questions.

One day, I did get too close. The Inspector told me that he was going to take me home to clean his house and wash his dishes. There was NO WAY I was going to go with him! Now I was scared. I ran and hid behind my dad. Later when The Inspector was gone, I told my dad what he had said. Dad reassured me that The Inspector would not take me home with him. But I was still scared and always stayed away from him.

Now Erv was the mechanic at my dad's shop. He was a very nice bachelor who my mom and dad would occasionally invite for lunch when Mom made my favorite German foods like *Knoepfla* and sauerkraut, *Käseknoepfla*, or borscht and dumplings. One late summer day Erv was sharpening silage cutter knives on the big automatic grinding machine. Sparks flew. The knives got very hot from the grinding. Erv wore gloves and used a heavy rag to handle the knives and lay them on the concrete floor to cool.

Erv had just installed a dull knife to sharpen when The Inspector walked in. He went right to the stack of knives. He asked if they were hot but didn't wait for an answer. Instead, he touched a freshly ground and very hot silage cutter knife and got a nasty burn. I watched all this from a safe distance, still scared but secretly glad. As a boy, I figured he'd gotten what he deserved.

After that, I didn't see The Inspector around the shop as often as before. I think he decided to do his "inspecting" at less dangerous places. I realize The Inspector was not a mean person. His wife had passed away several years earlier, and he was just a lonely old man with a very curious mind.

The Pleasure of Their Company

Sharon Chmielarz

Neighborhood ladies at farm auction sale, McIntosh County,
North Dakota, circa 1935.
(Photo courtesy of Carol Just)

Using one of its agents–
lamp or flare,

metaphor or window–
the sun, the master

of arousal, wakes me.

Then they appear.
They are here.
The grandmothers.

Coatless,
shadowless,
they stand

at my bedroom door
with the important question
for their granddaughter:

Hosh gut g'schlaffa?
"Did you sleep good?"

Grandmas Make Good Friends
Vicki Lynn Kempf Kurle

I lived with my parents in Aberdeen, South Dakota, in 1971, and had enrolled in nursing home administration at Presentation College. My dad's brother Herbert Kempf was the first male nurse to graduate from there. My dad, Joseph C. Kempf, was the administrator of the Bethesda Nursing Home in Aberdeen, and leased the Highmore and Bowdle nursing homes. During summer break from classes at Presentation, I worked at the Bowdle nursing home. I lived in a rented room. Sensing my need to become acquainted, my landlady took me along to her Mothers' Club. Lorraine Kurle, in her fifties, five feet tall, with natural curls and a fun spirit, attracted my attention with her joking stories about her "wild" boys, home from college for the summer. I'd see her most everywhere I went around town—at the bakery housed in the old bank, Ozzie's SuperValu where I saw a big jar of large black Greek olives, the Red Owl, the A&B Shop where my films were developed, and the Bowdle Butcher Shop for German sausage. She invited me to join her when she went to close-by farms for cream, eggs, and vegetables. I met many people who spoke the same German accent of my Aberdeen grandparents— Cheureka for Eureka, Chava for Java, and Hossmer for Hosmer!

Lorraine introduced me to her mother, Minnie Mauch Bader, and her mother-in-law, Rose Gross Kurle, and to the "wild" sons I'd heard her talk about. They all wholeheartedly included me in their family life. I had a wonderful summer. Fall came and I returned to Aberdeen and winter classes at Presentation.

I returned to the summer job in Bowdle the following year. The little town now held the added attraction of Lorraine's son Charles, who I'd met the summer before. I moved into an apartment that had a stove. My mom hadn't taught me much about cooking. I wanted to experiment with some

47

cooking on my own. My Norwegian mother made a dish she called "pasties." I'd watched her make it, and tried it. You fill circles of dough with hamburger, carrots, potatoes, and onions, fold in half, crimp the edges, and bake. When Lorraine heard about my interest in practicing cooking, she gave me some of the Mothers' Club cookbooks.

I loved spending time with the grandmas. During canning season, Grandma Bader and Lorraine worked together. I joined them and learned how to put up peaches, pears, tomatoes, bread and butter pickles, pickled beets, and strawberry-rhubarb jam. I didn't care for the dill watermelon pickles; the sweeter ones were better. Lorraine's basement held two refrigerators and two freezers (International Harvester brand) that were always full. Floor-to-ceiling shelves in the storage room held jars filled with the summer's bounty. One room held Charles's dad's work room. Their lifestyle was all new and exciting to me.

Lorraine's kitchen had floor-to-ceiling green cupboards and her walk-in pantry held antique items like a coffee grinder and crocks. The tea pot whistled on the stove. When Lorraine baked cinnamon and caramel rolls and buns, there were so many they covered the kitchen table, the green counter with metal edges, and the washing machine until they went into the freezer. I learned to cook more German food—*Halupsie*, strudels, *Knoepfla*, cheese buttons, cucumber salad, borscht, *Kuchen*, *Pfefferneusse* cookies. They made their own ice cream. I even got to crank the freezer.

I learned to embroider and cross-stitch from Lorraine. She hung two of my pictures in her living room. She helped me make a blue tie quilt. Lorraine's son Charles and I were dating regularly by then. I even sewed a lined burgundy suit jacket for him on his mom's sewing machine. I had a wonderful time. Lorraine's door was never locked. People selling Avon, Amway, and Watkins products would just walk right in! A key was always left under an embroidered cloth on top of the dryer in the enclosed back porch.

Grandma Bader tended the chamomile plants that grew next to the old-fashioned outside cellar door. Everyone liked chamomile tea except

Lorraine Bader Kurle stretching strudle dough, circa 1973.
(Photo courtesy of Vicki Lynn Kempf Kurle)

me. Hollyhocks and peony and lilac bushes grew along the south side of the two-story yellow house built in 1903. A round picnic table and a tall white Purple Martin birdhouse Charles's dad had built were outdoors. They washed their bread bags and hung them on the clothesline to dry. I loved using their wooden clothespins to hang my colored bikinis, bras, and halter tops—probably not a good idea. Grandma Kurle lived right next door and had a good view from where she sat by her large kitchen window. Before she first met me, she had warned her grandson Charles that she had heard I was wild.

Grandma Kurle had lived next door to Charles since 1951. She was a more serious type of person, but always had good stories to tell. She had written in small green diaries each day since the 1930s. Her *Kuchen* tasted like my grandma Ida Kempf's, and she made a lot of it. Her diary said six hundred one year.

She showed me how to make *Krautknoepf,* with hamburger, ham, onions, and sauerkraut wrapped in bread dough and baked in a roaster. She crocheted hundreds of doilies. When her eyesight began to fail, she made afghans. Before her stroke at age ninety-five, she made six afghans for us, (Charles and I had married) including two baby afghans. She passed away at age one hundred.

Grandma Bader lived upstairs in Lorraine's house. She had the whole upstairs—two bedrooms, living room, kitchen, and bathroom. Lorraine invited me to rent one of the bedrooms. Grandma Bader became very special to me. We often stayed up late talking, sitting on her double brass bed in her cozy bedroom, or on my twin beds. Each bedroom had a white pitcher and bowl on the dresser. Her large living room had yellow pine floors. The doors had raised panels with beautiful metal rose design antique knobs and tall platelets. I loved the old fashioned furnishings.

Yes, I became Mrs. Charles Kurle. His grandmothers and mother became lifetime friends. I learned so much from them. Their knowledge and guidance benefitted me all my life through.

CHAPTER THREE

$\mathcal{WAR}$

Karl Rennich in Russian military uniform, circa 1904/05.
(Photo courtesy of Merv Rennich)

Stay of Execution

Duane Maas

Peter Meidinger served in the 7th or 8th Army Corps of the Russian Cavalry from 1876 to 1881. He was arrested and charged with falling asleep at his post while guarding a bridge on assigned guard duty—a capital offense. Peter was subjected to a field court martial. Found guilty, he was sentenced to death by a firing squad.

The day of Peter's execution arrived. The members of the firing squad placed a sack over Peter's head and took their positions, ready for the order to fire. At that moment, a Russian officer on horseback came upon the scene and interrupted the proceedings, demanding to know why a Russian soldier was being executed. He listened to the details of the case and ordered the execution to be stopped. The firing squad dropped their weapons. The sack was removed from Peter's head. Peter had a stay of execution.

Why was Peter's life spared? His family knew he had participated in the Turkish campaigns of 1876 and 1878 when he was first drafted into the Russian army. Russia did not declare war on Turkey until April 1877, but they did send military officers in 1876 to help the Balkan countries in their rebellion against Turkish control. Could Peter have been a part of that?

Peter survived the war and returned to his family home in Kassel, a village in the Glückstal Colonies in South Russia, where he married Christina Gramm on November 23, 1881. They were blessed with thirteen children; however, as was common in that time, five died in childhood.

Russian Empire military history, including the Russian Cavalry, begins in 1721, when Czar Peter the Great established a military, to 1917, when the Russian Revolution led to establishment of the Soviet Union.

Peter and Christina (Gramm) Meidinger.
(Photo courtesy of Eugene Maas)

Peter and Christina, their eight surviving children, and Christina's mother immigrated to America in March 1903. They settled in Miller Township, Logan County, about six miles south of Streeter, North Dakota.

A half-century later Walter Maas, the husband of Peter's granddaughter Lydia Meidinger, heard Peter's Russian Cavalry stay of execution story from a Mr. Reuben who had known Peter. Apparently years earlier, Peter had told this story to his friend Mr. Reuben, but never passed it on to any of his own family members. At least, Walter never found anyone in the family who had ever heard the story. Walter passed the story on to his son Duane, Peter's great-grandson.

Naturally, the story stirred much speculation by Walter and other family members. Why did that Russian officer save Peter's life? There are a few possibilities. The officer, too, may have been of German descent. During that period of Russian history, many of the higher-level officers in the Russian army actually were Germans.

Duane (Walter's son) offered another explanation. Very few of the native Russian soldiers could read and write at that time. Peter was German and the German colonists had schools in their villages. Therefore, they could read and write. Many of the Russian officers valued anyone who had those skills. Even though Peter's knowledge of the Russian language may have been limited, his German language skills could have been in demand because of the large number of German officers in the Russian army.

It could be that the Russian officer was not convinced the offense—that Peter had actually fallen asleep at his post—merited the execution of a valuable soldier.

Speculation aside, if Peter knew or had some theory as to why he was spared, he either never told Mr. Rueben or Walter never heard that part of the story. Peter Meidinger's stay of execution remains a mystery to this day.

Ed. Note: This essay was written by long-time North Star Chapter member Duane Maas (1939-2016), great-grandson of Peter Meidinger, and submitted by his son Dan Maas. The original version appeared as a footnote in an autobiography by Lydia Meidinger Maas entitled *My Life - As I Remember It*, self-published in 2005. Additional information on the Meidinger family history can be found on a website created by Duane's brother Gene Maas at http://www.genemaas.net/Meidinger.htm.

The Cattle Car

Louise (Regehr) Wiens

Living near the busiest border crossing between Canada and the USA, we are among the thousands who cross regularly for shopping, entertainment, or travel purposes. Recently we were driving down an impeccable, busy boulevard in an upscale suburb of Detroit, Michigan, looking for a particular address, when I spotted it—a seemingly generic-looking, rather large, elongated red brick building. "Zekelman Holocaust Memorial Center" proclaimed the sign, and upon noticing it, I immediately implored my husband to pull over for a few minutes so that I could at least run in to check the hours of operation and maybe plan a visit in the near future, which he did.

It was an overcast summer's day as I entered the lofty front lobby where an elderly woman was manning the reception desk as a young man beside her appeared immersed in his computer. When I heard the shuffling of feet behind me, I turned to see a group of well-behaved and pensive school children being escorted on an organized tour of the center. My eyes continued to roam the expansive space around me. The woman recited her rehearsed yet informative speech to me about the center, and I, in response, divulged a few details of my family history to her, which I felt appeared to take her by great surprise. Then, from the corner of my eye to the left, I saw it, in the far side of the lobby. Without my glasses, I blinked. Then blinked again. A cattle car! Parked on wooden railway ties, a sign declared its authenticity and stated that it was a featured exhibit for the month. There, with my own eyes, I saw the chipped, wooden, painted sides with the tiny slats between them. There were the large rusted bolts on the outside, which ensured escape was not possible and, which I had heard, trapped inside both those living and those already dead. As the woman continued with her rehearsed rhetoric my tears began to flow, and I quickly exited the building.

Cattle Car (photo courtesy of Nancy Gertner)

It was in the fall of 1945 when my mother and her siblings were told that they would now have to leave Germany since "they were not born there." They had already been resettled more than once since being expelled from Bessarabia in the early 1940s and now once again they found themselves on the move. They were crowded into creaky wooden cattle cars, which appeared to no longer even be fit enough to hold even the animals that they had been built to contain. Yet this was human cargo, and along with ten other families who were also from her home village of Leipzig, the group made a pact to try to stay together as they once again faced an uncertain future. As the cattle cars departed, the former Leipzigers initially held out high hopes that they were returning to Romania, and they were already sensing the anticipation of the grape harvest and tasting the sweet fruit and the succulent wine. It was not long into the journey however, as the train made a sudden unexpected turn, that some of the older men on the trek with them, who were familiar with the rail system in place at that time, shared the shocking revelation with their fellow passengers that the train was indeed heading into another direction and that it was not to their beloved homeland.

Roll call was held randomly every few days as the train groaned to a squeaky halt and the masses of people were abruptly ordered to haphazardly jump out of the rail cars and risk injury by lunging onto the rocky steppe beneath to break their fall. The terrain appeared to show no signs of civilization, past or present. The gruff, uniformed Russian officer bellowed orders, seemingly oblivious to the shrieks of the frightened children who were clinging to the arms of their anxious mothers. With his starched cap perched impeccably on his head and his polished rifle by his side, he used intimidation tactics to try to calm down his newly recruited group of prisoners. Cold and disheveled, they were starting to succumb to malnutrition and exhaustion as they tried to pull themselves together for the sake of their children.

As my mother and her three-year-old son, Egon, took their allotted place in line, she began to mumble under her breath to the woman beside her about this surreal scene in which once again they had found themselves being involuntary participants. Aware that someone incredulously had the stamina to speak at the same time that he was barking instructions, the officer pivoted, pointing his rifle at my mother and her son and letting loose a string of Russian profanity. My mother was quickly silenced as the woman next to her, who understood Russian, translated that he threatened to send my mother to a place where she would never see the light of day again. "That quieted me and I knew then that I was in Russia," my mother had relayed to me many times over the years.

Anxiety and panic increased daily among the people and scuffles between them became common when on rare occasions the car doors would slowly creak open and a few handfuls of food would be thrown in as if one was feeding a flock of birds. The stench of excrement and human body odor of those living or those already dead was not easily absorbed by the mounds of dirty straw on which the deportees not only rested their heads but also used to garner some warmth. Sometimes the train was left abandoned on the tracks for days at a time, doors bolted from the outside, until days later the muffled distant chugs of the ancient and battered locomotive were the only indicator that the train was now on the move again. Fleeting glimpses of meager filtered light, peeking through the slits on the sides of the cattle car, illuminated the dust and the filth. The light was the only indicator of the time of day or night as people crowded near them to inhale some fresh air.

Weeks later the train had reached its destination of Martuk, Kazakhstan, where the exiled villagers were quickly pushed off and instructed to line up as officials from several local collective farms gathered to fill their work quotas by choosing from this new group of recruits. Women with children were considered a liability and usually not considered a popular pick, which resulted in my mother being separated from several of her siblings. The local nomadic groups of Kazaks were seemingly nonchalant to these newcomers, having apparently seen the pattern of forcibly relocated folks coming and going for many decades.

In 1955, after ten long years of exile, my mother, her new husband, their three-year-old son, Arthur, and several other family members were given permission from Moscow to return to Germany. At the eleventh hour, my mother was suddenly informed by the powers that be that a small complication had arisen in the form of her almost-nine-month pregnancy. She would not be able to leave after all, she was informed, as Russia was responsible not only for her well-being, but also for that of her soon-to-be-born child. "No one ever cared if we lived or died all those years," she often told me, "yet now, they suddenly acted as if they actually cared!" On a cold December day as the Siberian winds whipped fiercely, she was commanded to lie down wrapped in blankets in the back of an ox cart while a driver took her to a local doctor for an examination to ensure she would be able to withstand the journey home. "Unsuitable to travel," came the quick verdict from the intoxicated doctor, much to my mother's dismay. Yet undeterred, at the appointed time of day of the planned departure, she gathered with the others, determined not to be left behind again. Her family shoved her onto the train and hid her under a coat, as angry officials stormed the rail cars looking for the fully pregnant and defiant woman. As the train slowly started to move away from the station, the perception among the officials was that she was not present after all in the midst of this throng so very anxious to leave this Siberian wilderness behind, and they then dejectedly exited the train. Several weeks later the joyous home-comers arrived in Friedland, Germany, where safety, warm food, and lodging awaited them. After eating a banana, including part of the peeling, and drinking fresh coffee for the first time in ten years, my mother promptly went into labor, and delivered a full-term healthy baby girl at the hospital in Göttingen.

So it was that on that overcast June day as I stood in awe in that Holocaust Museum in front of that battered cattle car, words could never adequately describe the emotions that rocked my innermost being to the core. It was as if my two worlds had suddenly collided in front of me. You see, I was that baby, born so many years ago . . .

Previously published in the *North Star Chapter of Minnesota Newsletter*, Volume 40, Number 4, November 2015.

Draft Notice

Larry Kleingartner

Germans have a checkered history regarding going to war. Some historians label Germans as "war-like." There are plenty of reasons to agree with that label when you look at European history. During the American Revolution, Hessians (from the princely House of Hesse) were recruited as mercenary soldiers. Examples of Germans that challenge the "war-like" stereotype include Anabaptist groups founded in Switzerland and southern Germany. These religion-based groups are most commonly known as Amish, Mennonite, and Hutterite, and have suffered historically for their opposition to military service.

Larry Kleingartner with his mother, Elsie Riebhagen Kleingartner,
who had a significant impact on his view of military service, circa 1952.
(Photo courtesy of Larry Kleingartner)

Reasons for our ancestors leaving Germany for Russia usually include the economic devastation multiple European wars left on our relatives. The Russian promise issued by Catherine the Great's Manifesto in 1763 promising "no military service" obviously provided a sweet enticement to our German ancestors. The reneging of that promise in 1874 by Tsar Alexander II was certainly a significant reason our German relatives began to look beyond Russian borders for a new country.

What does this introduction to German militarism have to do with my German from Russia heritage and myself? First of all, it is important to point out that I had three sisters, but I was the only son, born in 1945. All four of my grandparents came from various villages in Bessarabia. None of my Bessarabian grandparents served in any military in Russia or the USA, nor did my father. My blood uncles on both sides made efforts to avoid serving in World War II. One uncle who had been drafted during WWII failed to report for duty and spent time in prison. Until he was apprehended, my father and grandfather aided and abetted him.

My growing-up years in a one-hundred-percent German from Russia family in south-central North Dakota was typical of most Germans from Russia families. This included hard work, church attendance, and no frills. I had one experience relating to the military that might have been different from other German from Russia sons. From my early years my parents, in particular my mother, would explain the ravages of *Krieg* (war). Her arguments centered on "poor folks fight the wars of the rich." On one particular occasion, at a movie theater, we watched a war newsreel before the main feature. As the short documentary unfolded on the screen, my mother grabbed my arm and said, "There will be a war when you are of age, but you will not be going." That pronouncement had a real impact on me at that young age of six or seven.

By the time I graduated from college in 1967, the Vietnam War was in full force. The military draft was impacting many of my high school and college classmates. I never considered enlisting. Two months after my college

A Hessian is an inhabitant of Hesse, a region in what is currently north-central Germany. Prior to unification of Germany in 1871 the territory of Hesse was occupied by the Grand Duchy of Hesse, the Duchy of Nassau, the free city of Frankfurt, and the Electorate of Hesse. The term Hesse derives from a Germanic tribe called the Chatti who settled in the area in the first century BCE.

graduation, my parents received my draft board notice requiring that I report to take my military draft physical. At that time I was working in western North Dakota, and it was difficult to reach me. But my parents made the long-distance phone call and my father, who was really quite passive, told me a packet from the county draft board had arrived. Signatures were required. We knew I faced the draft.

My father asked me what he should do with the mailing. While I stammered for a bit, my father interjected by stating that he would "burn the packet." I strongly encouraged him not to do that. My parents signed and sent the documents back, and then collected my health records relating to rheumatic fever that I had as a child. I took the records to the draft physical, but they got little consideration.

I had never seen my parents so motivated on a single issue. We were raised with expectations, but little interference in our private lives once we left home. Their gathering of my health records was significant. It was just something they ordinarily would not have done.

My question is: From where did this anti-war attitude come? It had to be beyond my parents' generation. It must have been a deep seated position going back to past generations. My parents admitted they often heard their parents talk of the scourge of war. Did it go back to Germany where so many wars were fought? Did it have to do with Napoleon's armies crossing their fields, taking their boys for war?

At the end of the day, a technicality exempted me from the draft. I joined the Peace Corps and spent two wonderful years in India making many friends and passing along the good will of the American people.

Many wars have since passed before me. I often think of the power of an extended hand as opposed to the end of a gun. This was certainly something I understood growing up in my German from Russia household.

CHAPTER FOUR

Out of the Farmyard, into the Schoolyard and Beyond!

Army Specialist 5th Class Ron Scherbenski,
Braumholder, West Germany, 1968.
(Photo courtesy of Ron Scherbenski)

Bauer #2 Launched a Lifetime of Learning

Ron Scherbenski

Our farm, just south and west of Eureka, South Dakota, was located in Bauer Township, one-half mile across the pasture from Bauer #2, our country school. I looked forward to going to school from an early age. Every year on the last day of school there was a picnic and the incoming students for the next year were invited. I awaited that event with great anticipation. The day before the big day I stepped on a board with a nail protruding that went through the bottom of my shoe and into my foot. I was unable to attend the picnic and was very disappointed. From our house, I could hear the students playing and having a good time. Sadly my first day of school had to wait until the fall of 1951.

My parents purchased our farm in 1944 and with it came a *Batsa* house. Instead of sod, it was made of a clay-straw mixture, formed into blocks, sun-dried, and stacked. It was an architecture style brought to America with the Germans who migrated from South Russia. The house was plastered on the inside and sided with wood on the outside. The walls were about thirty inches thick, cool in summer, warm in winter. Until we were connected to rural electricity in 1951, we used kerosene lamps. When I visited my ancestral villages Alexanderhilff and Hoffnungstal in Ukraine in 2003, I was the guest of a family whose house was of similar *Batsa* construction.

The day came when I went off to school with very limited English language skills. My first language was a *Schwäbisch* German dialect brought

---

Batsa refers to sun-dried bricks made of puddled clay. The bricks are shaped by pressing the clay into wooden molds ten to eighteen inches long. *Batsa* was typically used by Black Sea Germans. A common house style was one story with a loft and attached vestibule on the long side leading into the kitchen.

---

to America with my immigrant grandparents. Wanting to be prepared I asked Mom what I should say to my teacher when I arrived at school the first day. She told me to ask "Where do I put my dinner pail?" in English. You see, in our farm family we ate breakfast, dinner, and supper.

That first year Bauer #2 started out with five students until about two months into the school year when the Kramlich family moved to town. We were down to four students of varying grade levels for the rest of the year. Some years enrollment grew to as many as twelve students at one time. During my eight years at Bauer #2 all the students were able to speak our German dialect but we also got used to conversing in English. I remember a new first-grader commenting on my sister, saying *"Die isch sachrisch scha"* (She is damn nice-looking).

There was no indoor plumbing at our school so there was a girls' outhouse and a boys' outhouse. The girls had a three-holer and the boys had a two-holer.

South Dakota winters can be harsh. Normally during extreme weather I would get a ride to school, but one particular morning the thermometer read forty below and neither our car nor the truck would start. It was a bright, clear day, and dead calm. My parents waited until they saw the teacher's car at the school, bundled me up. and had me walk the one-half mile to school, watching me all the way to make sure I got there.

Recess was time to play games such as red rover, hide and seek, kick the can, and softball. When I was in fourth grade we got some playground equipment, two swings and two see-saws. This was a very big deal for us! At some point a basketball hoop was attached to the schoolhouse.

Our teacher when I was in third, fourth, and fifth grade was Mrs. Jundt. She had us say grace before dinner every day and we all thought it was an important event when "under God" was added to the Pledge of Allegiance sometime in the 1950s.

My sister joined me on the walk to and from school when I went into fifth grade. Going to school we would cut across the pasture but on the

Report card (Photo courtesy of Ron Scherbenski)

way home we followed the road. It was farther going by road but that way we got to walk with the Ottenbacher children for half the way. During good weather we would sit and talk at the mailbox which was where we went our way and they went theirs. Arnie Ottenbacher was my only classmate and best friend. We still touch base with each other on occasion and exchange Christmas letters. Roger Kramlich from those first two months of country school has reconnected with me on Facebook.

Bauer #3 closed when I was in fifth grade or so and the one remaining student from that school joined us in Bauer #2. He had to bring his own desk

The Pledge of Allegiance was introduced to public schools in the US in 1892. In 1951, the Knights of Columbus, the world's largest Catholic fraternal service organization, began including the words "under God" in the Pledge after a suggestion from an Illinois attorney who pointed out that the words were used by Lincoln in the Gettysburg Address. Several faith leaders lobbied Congress to have the words put in permanently, and President Eisenhower signed it into law in 1954.

because we did not have one that was the right size for him. It was a newer desk and the rest of us were envious. We students would travel to Bauer #4 in the fall for "Rally Day" and have athletic competitions. When I was in seventh and eighth grade Mr. Don Heupel was our teacher. He had been a high school athlete and I learned to do the high jump from him and won the competition. In the winter we went to Bauer #4 for academic contests that included math, spelling, and a declamation contest in which I did "Tom Sawyer Whitewashing the Fence." I did not get to represent the Bauer district at the spring county level contest.

When I was nearing completion of the eighth grade I was not at all sure I wanted to go to high school. It seemed so huge with over 200 students in grades nine through twelve. I could not see the need for education. After all, my parents only had an eighth-grade education and they were doing fine. My teacher tried to convince me that not going would be a mistake and even asked the County Superintendent, Otto Strobol, to stop by and talk to me about this. Mr. Strobol said that there was nothing wrong with being a farmer but if I wanted to do anything else, high school would open the door to more possibilities. I did go on to high school in Eureka and, of course, I was glad I did.

When I got to high school I realized that one of my concerns was that I was not as well prepared as the students that had gone to "town school." This proved not to be the case and I soon learned I could hold my own academically.

Upon graduation I attended Westmar College in LeMars, Iowa, for one year and decided that liberal arts was not for me so I transferred to Dunwoody College of Technology in Minneapolis and became an auto mechanic.

After graduation from Dunwoody I received my draft notice and found myself spending eighteen months serving in the US Army in Baumholder, Rhineland Pfalz, Germany. The military post was built for training Rommel's *Afrika* Corps and, as such, had very nice barracks and a huge tank training area. There I learned that my knowledge of German was very helpful in communicating with the local residents.

Upon returning to Minnesota I worked as an auto mechanic for ten years, followed by twenty-seven years as an automotive instructor at St. Paul College. A career highlight was a two-month sabbatical in 2004 in Germany to observe their apprenticeship program and shadowing some technicians working in dealerships. I also spent a week at a *Berufschule,* which is similar to our technical training centers in the USA. Again, my childhood first language served me well conversationally. Mastering the technical language was a bit of a challenge, but I did it.

I believe that my country school education at Bauer #2 and the dedicated teachers who taught there more than prepared me for a life of learning.

Berufsschule is a German vocational school that students may choose to attend after finishing secondary school. Students normally attend class twice a week during a two-to-four-year apprenticeship; the other days are spent working at a company. During the apprenticeship, the apprentice is a part-time salaried employee of the company. After passing the *Berufsschule* the student is awarded a certificate and is ready for a career up to a low management level.

71

A Farm School Education

Henrietta Weigel

Simply getting to school involved great time and effort. I remember walking with my younger sister, Kathy, to the country schoolhouse, which was located about a half mile from our farm north of Zeeland, North Dakota, in McIntosh County. To get there, we had to climb over two fences into the neighbors' property. We walked through pasture grass and across a plowed field, picking our way over prairie dog holes, furrows, and stubble. When the neighbors' Hereford cattle were grazing near our walking path, we walked around the outside of the fence, which added another half mile. We were terrified that their long-horned bull with a white face would run after us.

The schoolhouse itself was a simple two-story structure. Both the wood exterior and the plastered interior walls were painted white. The only windows were on the north side. There was no electricity or indoor plumbing, and the only source of heat was the wood and coal furnace, which piped in warm air from the basement through a large floor vent in the middle of the room. We crowded around the warm air vent when it was cold, setting our desks in a circle while we did our lessons. The outhouse was our only bathroom facility.

Students numbered about twelve to sixteen during my school years, 1948-1956, and the teachers taught all subjects in first through eighth grades. Most students only completed eight grades; then they usually left school to help work on their families' farms. The teacher was always busy assigning lessons, helping students with their assignments, grading papers, and making out report cards. She had to teach to many different ability levels, and there was no set curriculum from the school district. We learned the "Three R's": Reading, 'Riting, and 'Rithmetic. Those were the most important subjects to know at the time since most people would need those basic skills to make a living or keep running the family farm. However, we also studied some

72

Farm school students brought their lunches to school and kept them on the shelf until lunch time. (Photo courtesy of Nancy Gertner)

geography, citizenship, and early American history. We didn't do much art, music, or physical education. Students brought their own supplies from home, including pencils, paper, crayons, and rulers. Workbooks were provided by the school. We didn't have calculators for math.

I couldn't speak any English my first day of school—I only knew German because that's what Kathy and I spoke at home with our parents, Joseph G. Weigel and Elizabeth Therese (Malsam) Weigel. There were no libraries for us to go check out English children's books, and everyone living around us also only spoke German. My first-grade teacher, Miss Virginia Brandner, spoke both English and German, so she taught me how to speak English. I started by learning how to read and write the alphabet, and wrote my name for the first time. It was not customary for children to learn these skills at home with their parents. The common practice was that it was the teacher's job, not the parents', to teach children how to read and write in English. Parents considered it a waste of their time; they felt it was more important to develop the everyday skills needed to run the farm. After learning the alphabet, we started to read basic books like "Dick and Jane," "Mother Goose," and nursery rhymes. Miss Brandner was also my teacher for second, third, and fifth grade. My other teachers were Miss Laura Jundt for fourth grade, Mrs. Jacob Weisner for sixth grade, and Miss Veronica Seiler for seventh grade.

At recess time, we all played games together outside year-round, unless it was bitterly cold. Some of our favorites games were pump pump pullaway, hide and seek, tag, and softball. When there was snow on the ground, we played fox and geese. Playing games was challenging for me because I felt I didn't fit in very well. My sister and I, having no older brothers or sisters to play with us at home, weren't experienced with these games. I was usually the last one picked for a team, and because I was overweight, I wasn't as fast as the other students.

One memorable day at school, it was too cold to play outside during recess, so we went downstairs and played tag. It was a little dangerous because we ran around the furnace in the center of the room. As I was running from someone chasing me, I smacked right up against the cement wall with my right arm. Shooting pain went up my arm and I gasped, slipping slowly down the wall to the floor. I looked down and saw that my forearm was crooked where the bone was broken. My stomach turned. All the children stopped playing tag around the furnace and went upstairs so the teacher could comfort them. We had no telephone at the school, so my classmate Richard rode his Shetland

The *Dick and Jane* series was created in 1927. During the next five decades, eighty-five million American children learned to read with the book family comprised of Dick, Jane, Sally, Mother, Father, Spot (dog), Puff (cat), and Tim (teddy bear).

pony to our farm to inform my parents that I had broken my arm. My dad came right away and took me to the doctor in Eureka, South Dakota, about a twenty-five-mile ride. Pain shot through my arm every time I moved it and whenever the car went over a bump as we drove from North Dakota into South Dakota.

Finally we arrived at the doctor's office. To set my arm, Dr. McIntosh put one hand around the wrist and his other hand around the elbow in order to set the bone, then wrapped my forearm in cotton with a steel plate on one side to keep it straight. I watched as he soaked strips of plastered gauze in water and wrapped them around my arm to make a cast. He put my arm in a sling because the cast was heavy like cement after it dried.

Breaking my right arm, the one I used to write and eat, was very traumatic. Functioning with one arm was a new experience. I needed help doing the most basic things—getting dressed, washing my hair, and even eating. At school, I had to write with my left hand, which was slow and cumbersome. My handwriting was almost illegible. I also felt handicapped when trying to join in the games at recess.

After six weeks, I returned to the doctor's office to have the cast removed. I was afraid when Dr. McIntosh came in with a saw; I was sure he would cut my arm with it while removing the cast. But he said my arm would be safe because it was wrapped in cotton and the saw wouldn't cut cotton. My arm felt strange after the cast came off; all the heaviness and protection of the cast was gone. I felt like I had lost a security blanket and I was afraid my arm might not be healed yet. My arm was very pale from being covered by the cast for six weeks and there was lots of dead skin because the arm hadn't been bathed for so long. The arm was weak and there was no physical therapy so it took me a while to get confident using it again.

As I advanced to eighth grade with Miss Lorraine Wiest as my teacher, I was preparing myself for graduation. In order to fulfill the education requirements for the state of North Dakota, I had to take a final test. After the school year officially ended, all the eighth grade students stayed on for an extra two weeks to prepare for our final comprehensive exam. I had to review everything I had learned over the school year and then take the test, spread out over several days. After passing the exam, I received a certificate in the mail to document that I had completed my education from Farmers District #29, School #2, in McIntosh County, North Dakota.

My One-Room Schoolhouse
Lil Ward

I was the youngest of ten children, all of whom attended the Klein School, about ten miles south of Gackle, North Dakota. We called it the "farm school," which served students in first through eighth grades. I attended with three other siblings. I was pretty timid and scared. Aside from going to town on Saturday night and church on Sunday with Dad and Mom, school was the first time I really felt I was on my own. We usually got a ride to school but had to walk the mile and a half home. When I was small that was a long walk. My brother Pete was the one who took care of me when I got scared and carried me when I got tired.

My class had the same three kids for six years. There were typically ten to fifteen students from five to eight families in the eight grades. Some years there were no students for some of the grades. But I learned so much from the upper classmen as I listened to their assignments. I'm a pretty good speller and I think it's because I spelled the "hard" words that the older students had to learn and recite. It was much more fun than the "baby" words we were given. The same was true of math, but history I didn't like so much. Who cared about the rest of the world when mine was tied up with my family's world, which basically consisted of North and South Dakota? Just like church and Sunday School were your extended family, so were your fellow classmates and their families. That's where my world started and ended except for my many relatives.

Our one-room schoolhouse faced south with windows on the east side. Every day we started with the teacher or an older student raising the flag on the pole next to the school. Then we said the Pledge of Allegiance. Inside were blackboards on two walls. Everyone had to help with erasing the boards then taking the erasers outside to pound them together to clean them. The outhouses were behind the school, one for girls and one for boys. It seemed a long walk from the school to the outhouse, especially in sub-zero temperatures.

Some Fridays we helped clean the floor. The desks were pushed to one side and sweeping compound was tossed over the floor. The students, while wearing shoes, got to slide on the floor, which would clean it. After moving the desks and cleaning both sides of the room, the compound was swept up to use on another Friday cleaning day. It was a fun way to finish the week.

We brought our lunches from home using Karo syrup pails for lunch buckets. Our sandwiches were made with homemade bread and we envied the kids that had "store-bought" bread. We ate a lot of sandwiches made with peanut butter mixed with Karo syrup. That's still my favorite way to eat peanut butter.

There was a barn on the property that was mostly empty. The barn was in an open space so it was a great building to play ante-I-over around. A vivid memory as a young student was seeing the older boys kissing the older girls behind the barn. Oh my, do I tell the teacher? I don't think I ever told the teacher but I told my brothers and sister as we walked home. They probably let me know that tattling was not allowed. Later I caught them kissing behind the barn, too.

Of course, recess was our favorite time of the day. Some of the many games we played besides ante-I-over were tag (with the flag pole as home base), red rover, pom pom pullaway, kick the can, and kittenball (like softball, but played with a softer ball so we didn't need to use gloves). Teams for kittenball were picked after one of the captains held the bat and everyone stacked their hands on it. The last hand on the bat got to pick the first player for their team. It was nerve-wracking for me because I didn't want to be the last one picked for a team.

In December 1941, my dad sponsored his oldest sister, Elizabeth, her son and daughter-in-law, and their four children to come to America from Germany, where they had moved from South Russia. Hitler had relocated them to Poland and then to Germany. The children stayed with us. It was a really harsh winter. One day after a very heavy snowstorm, my dad put the hayrack on skis pulled by horses to take the kids to school. Dad wouldn't let me go along because I was too little. I stood by the big kitchen window with tears streaming down my face watching Dad drive off with the older kids. I wanted so badly to go on that sleigh ride.

Another time my sister Helen, my cousin Inge, and I couldn't go to school because of a blizzard but it turned into a beautiful sunshiny day. Helen and Inge snuck outside, got two pairs of skis, and skied a mile to the Apostolic Finnish Lutheran Church, called the Finn Church and used for a local landmark, and waited for the boys to come home from school. They hid from the boys intending to scare them but Pete and Ed got a ride to the church instead of walking so they spotted the girls. The boys took the skis away from them and skied home so the girls had to walk back. When the girls got home they tattled on the boys but got in more trouble because they weren't supposed to be out there anyway. They never got to stay home from school again.

We had parties at school for many events. My mom was often there helping with Halloween, Christmas, and end-of-year picnics. We forgot lessons as we played games, had treats, and sometimes had a program. I am lucky that Mom had a camera so I have a few pictures of the kids of Klein School.

Mom donated an old organ to the school, and my teacher in fourth through sixth grade, Mrs. Krieger, loved music. Sometimes during the winter months at recess she would allow the students to push their desks to the side of the room. A couple of the guys could play the organ by ear, mostly polkas and waltzes. Many of us learned to dance at Klein School during recess. If we didn't obey the teacher we wouldn't get dance lessons for a while. I often wonder what happened to Mom's old organ when the school closed.

We moved into Gackle after my dad died suddenly. I was scared and town school was pretty overwhelming for me. Starting in junior high I had to

Klein School, front row: Dennis Muonio, Aaron Suko, Lil Kleingartner Ward; middle row: Karen Buerkle Miller, JoAnn Buerkle Miller, Helen Kleingartner, Beulah Schlecht Kruse; back row: Harry Lippert, Edwin Kleingartner, Melvin (Pete) Kleingartner, Darrell Lippert. (Photo courtesy of Lil Kleingartner Ward)

move from room to room for classes in this big building which also housed the high school. The kids were nice to me but there were so many of them. Thrown into "the real world" was hard but I toughened up quickly. I got involved with activities and made friends who also helped me with the studies

I didn't understand. There weren't as many subjects taught at the farm school since the teacher had to teach all subjects to all grades in one room. I missed listening to the lessons of the upper classmen. I missed the camaraderie of eating and playing with my friends. When I was a freshman, my Klein School classmates and Sunday School friends joined me in high school.

The Klein School closed in 1960 and the building was used as a voting place for many years before being purchased by former student Ardell Schmidt. He moved it a few hundred yards, took out the windows, put a big door in front, and used it to store machinery. The original school foundation and crumbled steps are still on the original site but the barn and outhouses are gone. The blackboards are still intact, but when I asked Ardell about any leftover books, he said all the "good" books like *Dick and Jane* were taken and the others had probably been chewed by mice. He gave me permission to go and take a look but since the dirt floor is uneven because of all the machinery that drove over it, I haven't done that yet.

Trees

Bernelda Kallenberger Becker

M r. Werre's assignment had been to memorize poet Joyce Kilmer's "Trees." As I stood beside his desk in the one-room country school, my eyes surveyed the treeless plains through the schoolhouse window and I recited in a monotone voice . . .

> "I think that I shall never see
> A poem as lovely as a tree."

My father had planted Russian olive, plum, and chokecherry trees to shelter our farm from the raging winter blizzards. They were sparse and scraggly. They only fit my definition of lovely when they had sweet-smelling blossoms in early spring. My third-grade mind struggled with the meaning of the words as I droned on . . .

> "A tree whose mouth in summer pressed
> Against the earth's sweet flowing breast."

What did a chicken breast have to do with the earth? My mother said Daddy always ate the choice piece of the chicken, the breast, because he worked hard in the field and deserved it.

The eighth-grade boys giggled when our class read that line out loud. Why were boys always so dumb and made fun of stuff, I wondered. I had asked Mr. Werre to explain. He said the poet had meant the roots of the tree draw water and nourishment from the damp earth. Damp earth? We hadn't had rain for six weeks, and Daddy said if it didn't rain soon there would be no crop this year. I continued, mumbling . . .

> "A tree that may in summer wear
> A nest of robins in her hair,"

The robins in our yard built nests on flat surfaces, usually under an eave. A barn swallow flew past the window on its way to the schoolhouse barn. It was probably carrying something it could use to build its nest in the rafters. Daddy showed me a meadowlark nest once—they build their nests on the ground. What a dumb poem, I thought again. I sighed and went on to the finish . . .

"Poems are made by fools like me
But only God can make a tree."

Finally a part of the poem that made sense. I knew about fools. Daddy grumbled all the time about the fools who didn't understand what President Roosevelt was trying to accomplish. And even I know it takes God to make our scraggly trees.

I took my seat on the reciting bench at the front of the room, wiping my sweaty palms on the skirt of my dress. Whew! That was over. Bored as I listened to the next student's recitation, my eyes again strayed to the window. The swallow soared past on another trip to the barn. I loved school, but back then, memorizing poems I couldn't understand seemed like a waste of time to me.

Years have passed, and I've lived beneath hardy oaks and watched the squirrels enjoy their acorns. I've marveled at the beauty of crimson maples and savored maple syrup. I've inhaled the fragrance of an evergreen forest and harvested pinecones for holiday decorating. A robin nests on the lower limb of my flowering crab tree.

I've often caught myself reciting "Trees" through the years, as well as other poems I memorized and couldn't comprehend back then. Maturity has brought understanding and appreciation, not only of the poetry, but also of the poets. Thank you, Mr. Werre, for assigning poems to memorize.

Our New Ulm Vacation

Henrietta Weigel

We went on our first and only family vacation in 1954. We traveled to New Ulm, Minnesota, to visit Grandpa George and Grandma Mary Weigel, who had recently moved there from Zeeland, North Dakota. At this time, we also visited Dad's brother Uncle Louie, Aunt Mary, and our first cousins Arley and Fred, who also lived in New Ulm. We stayed with the grandparents for one week. Dad had a brand-new gray and white Chevrolet BelAir four-door sedan; it was the first car he ever owned that had an automatic transmission. In those days, cars didn't have seat belts, so we crammed four adults and three children into the car: Ma, Dad, Uncle

Blue Grotto in West Bend, Iowa. (Photo courtesy of Marcia Gertner Johnson)

Eugene, Aunt Annie, our cousin Shirley, Kathy, and me. We spent many hours driving. My dad was very strict, so we were supposed to stay quiet and act like the adults in the car. We were pretty well behaved so all he had to do was give us "the look" and we would obey. Ma and Aunt Annie packed a picnic dinner, snacks, and water and we occasionally stopped to buy gas and take potty breaks. We made the trip in one day, leaving early in the morning and arriving around suppertime. It was unheard of to stay in hotels or eat in restaurants when visiting relatives. They would have been offended if we hadn't accepted their offer to stay in their home.

One evening after my uncle got home from work, friends of Uncle Louie and Aunt Mary invited us to see their chinchilla farm. The chinchillas were kept in the basement of the house. Since they were pretty smelly, the owners had to keep the basement well ventilated. There were cages stacked on top of each other from floor to ceiling and from one side of the room to the other. To us children, it looked like there were hundreds of chinchillas but in reality there were maybe about one hundred. Chinchillas weren't raised to be pets; there was no emotional attachment, similar to the way we viewed our animals on the farm. They were simply raised to supplement a family's income. Since fur of the chinchilla is very dense and soft, the fur was used to make fur collars for ladies' expensive winter coats.

We also visited several sights during our stay in New Ulm. We went to the Hermann Monument, which had a tall spiral staircase. It went all the way to the top where we could see all of New Ulm and the Minnesota River valley. We also visited the Schell's Brewery, which was founded by the German immigrant August Schell in 1860 and has been kept in the family. We toured the brewery and saw how they brewed and bottled a special kind of beer called bock. After the tour we got a sample of the beer along with pretzels to eat.

We also visited the Way of the Cross Catholic Cemetery. More elaborate than a normal cemetery, it has the fourteen Stations of the Cross along a brick path that started at the entrance to the cemetery. Each station had realistic figures that showed a scene from Jesus' journey to the cross. It was unique for us to see the Stations of the Cross outdoors because we were used to seeing them at our church in a much smaller size. Now our Weigel grandparents, along with our aunt Elizabeth and her husband, Douglas Corcorn, are buried there.

For our final day trip we went to West Bend, Iowa, to see the Grotto of Redemption. It has since been listed in the 2001 National Register of Historic Places. Going inside the grotto was like going into a cave. It was gorgeous, like walking into a dream full of different colors and incredible detail. We had never ever seen anything like it. Gems and stones of different colors, shapes, sizes, and textures were set into the walls of the cave. Father Dobberstein began the project in 1912 as a dedication to the Virgin Mary and worked on it for forty-two years. Many years went by as he worked on the project because getting the stones and gems at that time required much effort. He sent letters to locate the desired stones and gems, had them brought over on a ship, and hauled by train. At the end of the day trip to Iowa we went back to our grandparents' house for supper and to enjoy another day before heading back home to North Dakota.

Looking back, I realize that this vacation was a once-in-a-lifetime experience for me. It was the one and only vacation I had where my dad was present. It was a very educational experience because of the different sights I saw, but it was also special to spend time with my family, riding in my dad's first brand-new car, living out of a suitcase, being in New Ulm for the first time, and enjoying my grandparents' hospitality.

Radio: Bringing the World to the Prairie

Bernelda Kallenberger Becker

Mama and I would hurry to finish the noon dishes and have the house neat. Then we settled down before the Philco car-battery radio in the kitchen. For a short few minutes in our busy day we could depart our mundane world and listen to the exciting problems of Ma Perkins and her family. If memory serves me right, my mother sometimes sneaked a package of Oxydol laundry soap, the product they advertised, into her grocery purchase on Saturday night. It made a nice change from her homemade lye soap.

Through the years, Sunday evening radio fare at our house always included Jack Benny. I can still sing the ad: "J-E-L-L-O" and hear announcer Don Wilson's voice, adding "Five delicious flavors!" We enjoyed this delicious treat in the fall, when the weather cooled enough for Jell-O to set if we put it outside. You see, we did not have an icebox and no electricity for a refrigerator.

We never missed *Fibber McGee and Molly,* and waited eagerly to hear things fall out when Fibber opened the closet door. How could one forget Digger Odell, the morose friendly undertaker when he used the expression: "I'll be the last guy to let you down." The Johnson Wax they advertised kept Mama's linoleum floors shining. Sometimes when she waxed the floor, she had me sit on a scatter rug and pulled me back and forth to enhance the shine.

Radio in the 1930s and 1940s brought the world to the prairie. It had an impact on our lives. Advertising slogans heard then are embedded in my brain. I have no trouble recalling "Call for Philip Morris" or "Lucky Strike means fine tobacco." As far back as then the cigarette companies tried to convince the listeners to "Try it, you'll like it."

Radio contributed to my spiritual self, too. Due to frequent moves during my early teens our family did not attend church. Being of a religious

Radio made by Jensen Radio Manufacturing of Chicago, founded in the 1920s.
Radios with a domed housing were very popular in the 1920s and 30s.
(Photo courtesy of James Gessele)

bent, I made up for the lack to my spiritual growth by listening to Dr. H. B. Fuller's *Old Time Revival Hour.* I sent several long letters to Dr. Fuller telling him my problems. I don't remember receiving a reply. I didn't really expect one. I had no money to send to help keep his program on the air—why would he spend a three-cent postage stamp on me? Just getting things off my chest helped.

I'm ashamed to admit I didn't have much interest in the news programs during those years, but at news time the radio was off-limits to me. My father would turn the dial to WNAX in Yankton, South Dakota, to hear the news. Naturally, we family members listened too. There were mainly three ways to keep informed on World War II news—radio, the Aberdeen newspaper, or the newsreels at the local movie theater. My only opportunity to go to a "show" was on our Saturday night shopping trip to town.

My dad was a staunch admirer of President Franklin D. Roosevelt. Everything stopped when FDR was scheduled to give one of his radio "fireside chats." We pulled our kitchen chairs up close to the radio to hear him report how things were going in World War II. He encouraged us citizens by telling us we had nothing to fear but fear itself. FDR was president for most of my growing-up years.

My parents had another program that took precedence to my preferred programs—when Lawrence Welk's band appeared on WNAX. Lawrence had grown up in Strasburg, North Dakota, so he was one of our own—a German from Russia who had made it in the world! My parents and a neighbor couple took a weekend and traveled to Yankton to dance to his music. Mother came home with a fancy dress she had purchased while there. She packed it in a trunk. It was too "floozy" for our staid community. I never saw her wear it.

In my late teens, a favorite program, *Your Hit Parade* sponsored by Lucky Strike cigarettes, found me before the radio with the current *Hit Parade* magazine on my lap. This magazine highlighted the most popular and best selling songs of the week. The announcer would announce which song would be played and sung next. I quickly located the lyrics in my magazine and sang along, memorizing the melody and words.

It's now 1949. I'm a young bride, aged twenty-one, married to a young farmer. My husband, home from the war, had been everywhere and I had been nowhere. I was ashamed of my German from Russia heritage. Hadn't Hitler been responsible for the European war? My parents had grumbled because the government had caused our only German newspaper to shut down because of censorship to make sure they weren't printing German propaganda. The government had also decreed our local pastors refrain from preaching sermons in German. The pastors did this because many of the elderly congregants still had difficulty with the English language.

Young and inexperienced, living in prairie country, I felt acutely aware of my lack of sophistication and culture. Where could I get it? I had been raised on polkas and schottisches, learned to dance at the local dance hall we called "The Hog Rassle" or at an occasional barn dance. One day, before I plugged in my iron, I flipped the dial on our radio and came across a station playing classical (long hair) music. Determined to improve myself, I made myself listen whenever I could, whether I liked it or not.

We moved to Minneapolis, Minnesota, in 1951. Television had not yet made its way to Aberdeen, South Dakota, at least not to our house or the houses of our friends. Imagine our shock when we visited the homes of our new friends. They had televisions in their living rooms. How could they afford such a luxury? Our prairie ways had followed us to Minneapolis. Determined that a radio was good enough for us, we purchased a chest freezer and filled it with half a beef purchased at the locker plant. My husband's co-workers tauntingly asked him, "Are you going to sit in your basement and watch your freezer?"

We broke down and purchased a seventeen-inch Admiral television eight years later so our three-year-old son could watch Captain Kangaroo. You know the rest, right? We've been hooked ever since.

CHAPTER FIVE

Down the Old Wurst and Knoepfla Lane

Fry sausage ready to be cooked. (photo courtesy of Carol Just)

A New View

Kristine Lamp

Have I ever lived in North Dakota? No. Am I a descendent of German from Russian heritage? No. What business do I have in writing about my impressions of North Dakota? I will tell you this: On my first visit to that state my experience became etched in my memory, and it remains unforgettable to this day. Let me explain.

Many years ago I accompanied my husband, Hank, on his business trip to North Dakota. I expected to see large barren areas with small towns sprinkled in between. That was a major misconception, for as we entered the state, lush fields of green flourished before us as far as the eye could see. As the road curved, the sight before me took my breath away. There in front of us appeared a beautiful, expansive blue lake. It was not a lake at all but an enormous field of azure-blue blooming flax. I was stunned. "We must pull over here, Hank, and take in this incredible scene." To this day I cannot forget it.

We drove on to a town where Hank made a business call. As he entered the office of the contractor, I heard the owner's greeting.

"Well, hi there, Hank! Come on in. I have some plans to show you."

"Good, Goldie, I'm anxious to see what we can do."

I waited in the car, and when the meeting was over, I heard these parting words, "We'll see you tonight, and bring the Mrs. to our house for some dinner." My, I thought, that's unusual to be invited for dinner after a short business call.

When we arrived at Goldie's home, the openness and hospitality amazed me. "Come on in, Hank, and here's your lovely bride. So good to meet you, Kris, and how nice you came with Hank this trip." The delicious aroma from the kitchen made me extra hungry. Goldie's wife came out and clasped my hand. "How nice of you to come to North Dakota, and how pleased we are that you came to our home. Dinner's not quite ready, but let's sit and visit first."

This was not an isolated incident. In most every town where Hank made a business call we were treated like royalty, invited into homes, or taken out to dinner. We formed new friendships that gave me a new perspective and respect for North Dakota people. I saw in them a genuine interest in us that was sincere and giving.

I now understand the origin of that true hospitality and culture. It arose from those first German immigrants who came from Russia to settle in this area seeking a new life, only to find loneliness, isolation, and little in the way of a welcome. They turned that around and opened their hearts and their homes to all those who followed. They knew only too well the difficulties encountered in adjusting to the new land.

Has the image of that enchanting field of sky-blue flax in full bloom dimmed over the years? Absolutely not, for I can merely close my eyes and see it again in all its splendor. Equally etched in my memory is the experience of the beautiful graciousness in the hearts of the North Dakota people. It lives on from the enduring example set by the very first German immigrants. What a wonderful heritage to leave behind!

Green Pepper Soup

Sharon Chmielarz

Memory is . . . an instrument for exploring the past('s) . . . theatre.
—Walter Benjamin

The wind has died down, and streets are made golden and splendid by fallen cottonwood leaves. Fall is here.

A pot of soup simmers on my stove. Green pepper soup, a variation on stuffed green peppers. I made up the recipe; today its flavor is the taste of comfort. And a lot easier to put together than stuffed peppers or *Halupsie*—stuffed cabbage. For it's true, whatever the ethnic group or culture, if you lose its

Ready for the pot. (Photo courtesy of Nancy Gertner)

special foods, you've lost where you come from. And it's faster to connect to the past through food. Alimentary. No travel necessary.

If space were time in North and South Dakota, it'd be fair to call wind and the prairie eternal, and the sky a fast-moving clock of ever-changing clouds. Leaves from a cornfield's blond-brown stalks swirl into the air like flocks of pale birds rising into an atrium. Soup is essential in this weather.

My soup has a tendency to stick on the pan's bottom despite my spraying the pot with Pam and a generous dose of olive oil. The burn is a mixture of hamburger and rice. I never add salt to my homemade soup. I figure there's enough flavoring in the added basil, bay leaf, canned tomato sauce, and dill. The part of Russia my German foreparents came from added cinnamon to chicken noodle soup, but cinnamon just wouldn't taste right with green pepper.

In the restaurant beside the Prairie Rose Motel in Edgeley, North Dakota, I heard the cook, a teenage blonde, mumble, "Anyone can bake an apple pie." Not so. And not anyone can make stuffed peppers the way my mother did. She could have made a fortune had she owned a little restaurant in the Twin Cities.

A rich fragrance of fresh green peppers begins to invade my house. I love that. It may be overpowering for others, but I don't mind the scent. It's all in what you get used to, like when everyone believes green peppers stink up the house, then it's harder for someone to disagree. That little doubt in someone's heart which raises its hand or clears its throat is shunted to the side. It has to get really loud before it's heard. But I like it.

My pot of soup will last me at least four days, for I'm a widow, dreadful title. It won't matter to me if the bottom burns a bit since I like to scrape the burned layer off and eat it. It has an intense taste of oil and soot. I wouldn't serve it to anyone, not even my sisters, though that might result in an unexpected surprise—we three coming together over great distances and finding another commonality in our blood—we like the taste of suffering.

On my journey, as some denominations call it, through life, I've brought with me the occasional craving for green pepper soup. It represents the best of the people I journeyed away from. It's plain and unadulterated. You've got to let it simmer on the stove for hours before the full flavor blends. It's impossible to be phony eating green pepper soup, and it isn't something to serve a sophisticated crowd unless they're interested in plain foods from rural regions. Its odor fills the house with a scent that hangs around for days in winter when windows are kept closed. But it's a part of me I recognize; since I, like most people, hunger at times for the familiar, even if I have to scrape it up. Soup is, after all, my choice of comfort food. It lasts a long time, like one tender, understanding glance.

Teeth

Bernelda Kallenberger Becker

I've been noticing teeth lately—beautiful teeth—white teeth. Not only the beautiful teeth of television news reporters and screen stars, but the teeth of ordinary people—people that aren't movie stars or models. You'll see them interviewed in news broadcasts or seated in program audiences. They have almost perfect teeth. Remarkable!

I can't help but compare them to people of my age group. We're the ones who survived the Great Depression—pre-orthodontists, pre-television and glossy magazine advertising. Any perfect teeth you'll find in our mouths are probably dentures. If we are fortunate enough to have our own teeth, we either have too many or not enough or you'll find them yellowed and stained. When our mouths open wide to laugh at your joke, you'll glimpse sparkling, shiny gold fillings. Some of us go through our "golden" years gumming it.

Does anyone in this day and age ever have a toothache? When did you last hear a parent threaten to pull a tooth by tying a string around it, then tie the other end of the string to a doorknob and slam the door? With all of our present-day advertising, could there possibly by anyone in the United States totally unaware that there are such things as toothpaste and toothbrushes?

Welcome to the world of my childhood—sans modern-day advertising. I can't recall seeing or hearing personal hygiene items advertised. I didn't know such products existed, and if I had, I would have had no money to spend on such frivolous items. The soap opera Mother listened to on the car-battery radio in the kitchen advertised Oxydol laundry soap. She understood and fought "ring around the collar," but the once-a-week bath in the washtub sufficed for our personal grooming as far as she was concerned. She had to carry water uphill from the well to the house,

Bernie Kallenberger, age 9.
(Photo courtesy of Bernelda Kallenberger Becker)

and back out again in a slop bucket after it was used. We used it sparingly.

I had my first visit to a dentist when I was a freshman in high school. By this time I had lost several teeth. He decided to do a filling. I'll never forget gripping the arms of the dental chair in fear while he pounded the filling into the cavity with a little wooden mallet.

The home economics teacher taught us freshman girls personal grooming. It was the first time I'd been given instruction on brushing teeth, filing fingernails, and brushing hair. I went to the drugstore and purchased a can of dry toothpowder and a toothbrush. But alas, the instruction came a bit too late for me and I had dentures by the time I was twenty-eight years old.

I'm happy for all those with perfect white teeth. I'm thankful for orthodontists. I'm glad we're more educated and aware of the need for brushing and flossing—wouldn't change it. But I'm also thankful there were skilled dentists who made it possible for us oldsters to go through life able to chew our food well, and to not be afraid to smile. And say, it ain't all bad to drop 'em into a bowl to soak overnight either—at least I don't have to floss.

Typical Wash Day on the Farm

Kathy Weigel

It was a Monday morning and I was at the kitchen table eating my oatmeal and fresh buttered bread. Suddenly I heard Ma yell from outside, "Hurry up with your breakfast, Kathy! It's time to get started with the wash." I groaned. It was Monday and we had to wash all the clothes, sheets, and towels again. I finished my oatmeal and gulped down my milk. It was time to get moving.

I really didn't feel like going outside to carry water to the house from the well, which was quite a distance away. But I didn't complain because I didn't want a lecture from Ma about talking back to adults. So I grabbed my bucket from the storage shed and headed out to the well. Ma and I carried three-gallon pails of water that felt like they weighed at least a ton all the way up a long hill to the house. By the fourth trip I was getting pretty tired so I sat down in the grass and started playing with the dog. Before too long, Ma came out and saw me. She said, "Get to work, Kathy! No time to rest! The wash needs to be done by supper because the neighbors are coming over to play pinochle." I pulled myself up and brought the last bucket to the big oval-shaped wash boiler in the basement. The water had been heating in the wash boiler on top of a kerosene stove so I tried not to splash myself as I poured the last bucket in.

Ma and I transferred the hot water from the wash boiler to the wringer wash machine. Then we added homemade lye soap, which had been made with lye, melted fat, and pork cracklings. Before adding the soap to the washtub we melted it on the stove. Since the water was very hot we used a stick to get the clothes out of the washtub and run them through the wringer. Ma said, "Be careful, you don't want to run your hand through the wringer along with the clothes!" I hadn't ever gotten my hand in the wringer but the stick had gone through multiple times. When that happened, the

Wringer washer at the American Historical Society of Germans from Russia Museum, Lincoln, Nebraska. (Photo courtesy of Nancy Gertner)

wringer would open and we would have to run the clothes through it again. Once all the clothes had been washed Ma added bluing to the water. Bluing was a whitening agent that was used only for clothes that you wanted to be bright white. We used it for our blouses and Dad's dress shirts. Once we were finished with the wash I carried the water up the stairs and outside, where I dumped it on the ground a few yards from the house.

Ma and I took the wash outside to hang it on the line to dry since we didn't have a clothes dryer in the house. I thought about how glad I was it wasn't winter! I remembered how freezing cold my hands would get when I had to take off my mittens in order to hang and pin the wet clothes on the line. I always wanted to run inside to warm them up but Ma always told me I had to wait until we were all done. I recalled how the clothes would be frozen stiff when Ma and I brought them inside to thaw before hanging them up.

A wringer mechanism with a washing machine was first patented in 1843. Electric washing machines were available in 1904, but were not generally present in rural homes until rural electrification projects were completed. Domestic washer production was suspended in the US during WWII; therefore, many rural homes didn't receive electric washers until the post-war era.

But now the sun was high in the sky and there was a nice breeze. The clothes would dry fast in this weather.

It was late morning by the time we had hung everything on the line so we went back into the house to get noon dinner on the table. My sister, Henrietta, had already prepared the chicken and boiled the potatoes, and Ma mashed the potatoes and fixed the gravy. I set the table and we sat down to eat as soon as Dad came in. All of a sudden we heard the cows mooing in the yard and the dog barking outside the window. "Uh oh," I said. "I wonder if the horseflies are bothering the cows again." It was late summer, and the horseflies would often bite the cows causing them to run under the clothes fluttering on the clothesline in order to chase the flies away. Dad got up and went to the door and I followed him. Sure enough, the cows were running through the yard with their tails in the air. They had gotten caught in the hanging laundry and had broken the clothesline. All of the clothes had been ripped off the line and were all over the ground getting stomped on by the cows. Dad whistled to the dog so he could chase them out of the yard. I went outside and looked at all the clean laundry on the ground, not so clean anymore.

I looked at Ma and said, "Ei, yei, yei, those darn cows!"

"Well," she said, "we can't cry over spilt milk. Let's get to work." And we had to start the process all over again!

A Childhood Visit to My Grandparents' House
Vicki Lynn Kempf Kurle

"We're in Aberdeen!" I exclaimed. We'd driven for three days in our sky-blue 1956 Chrysler, my mom and dad in front, food and snacks in tin lunch boxes and thermos jugs, and little brother Greg, six years old, and me, eight, in back. I had my coloring books, paper dolls, Etch A Sketch, and my favorite "magic slate" with its opaque erasable sheet that crackled when lifted. Aberdeen—where I was born!

"There's their house!" I cried excitedly—a white two-story with green trim and a white picket fence and hollyhocks and pink and red peonies at the curtained bay window. A tractor tire with blue and red painted treads bloomed with red petunias. On the narrow sidewalk to the back porch I walked missing the cracks. "They're pigeons," Dad said about the gray and white birds fluttering in cages. "He probably keeps them at the farm."

"WICKI!" Grandpa called, smiling from the squeaky screened door. I noticed his straight teeth because mine were crooked. He wore bib overalls. Grandma wore a flowery apron, big black thick shoes, and crinkled stockings. Her legs were thin. Her head looked small because her hair was pulled back tight.

Wicki. Why didn't my handsome grandpa learn how to say the "V"? But I really liked their accent. Dad explained we weren't German and not Russian but together. German was like hearing secrets I couldn't understand. I only knew one German word—*Dummkopf*—and the German table prayer we said before supper, *Abbe Lieber Vater Amen.*

Grandpa and Grandma met at a barn dance in Coldwater, North Dakota, where Grandpa played the violin in his band. Grandma Ida said he could always tell her apart from her twin, Lyda. Grandma said she probably was diabetic from having ten kids. "My back side," she said, "should be in the front and my tummy in the back." She let me watch while she gave herself shots in her upper legs. I didn't like watching my mom, an LPN nurse, give shots to the residents of the nursing home where my dad was administrator because it looked like jabbing.

While everyone else was talking, I was drawn to the living room's carved hidden sliding doors. I was having fun sliding them when Grandma said, "Let's just leave these open for now." She didn't look mad.

All Grandpa and Grandma's children's pictures were in big frames on the wall above the davenport. My dad's was of him and his accordion when he was on the radio station at age seventeen with Myron Floran. Gust Jr. was shown in the boxing ring where he won awards. Edna was a model and wore a fur shawl with claws on it. Ella was sitting in her beauty shop in Ellendale, North Dakota. Jeannie wore her nurse's uniform and hat. Herbert was in uniform as the first male nurse at Presentation College. Roy was in his military uniform. Harley and Paul were in their barber shops.

Grandpa kept his large drum with a foot pedal, his violin, and accordion in the living room. Grandpa's organ stood against the wall with the picture of Jesus knocking on the wood door. I loved hearing Grandpa and my dad singing and playing "Du Du Liegst Mir im Herzen," "Immer Noch ein Tröpfchen," and "Oh! Susanna." Grandma sang along sometimes, but she didn't have a singing voice. I could sing "Me and My Teddy Bear" and "The Teddy Bear's Picnic" to the record they gave me.

Grandpa's rolltop desk in the front hallway lured me, too. All the little drawers. I was one to sort through and rearrange, but Grandpa said, "Don't organize my papers. And leave everything in the drawers." I saw some of my letters I'd sent them. They always started out, "How are you? I am fine."

Off the entry was the stairway to upstairs. I went up and down on the steps' dark wood with my Slinky. And I snooped in my grandparents' large bedroom. It had a three-way mirror and a large brush and comb where Grandma brushed her hair each night. I looked in every drawer and saw lots of crocheted hankies. She had many round hatboxes on the floor. There was a

Gust Kempf playing instruments, circa 1960.
(Photo courtesy of Vicki Lynn Kempf Kurle)

trunk full of linen. Quilts hung from a quilt rack. A white chenille bedspread with pink flowers and green stems covered their soft beds.

Grandma wore a nightgown for sleeping and a nightcap just like in the Santa Claus storybooks. Her head looked tiny with her hair up in bobby pins. She kept her teeth floating in a clear plastic glass on her end table! We knelt down beside the bed to say prayers just like my dad did.

"Time to help me in the kitchen," Grandma would call. I liked putting her thick-sliced homemade bread on the antique slide out toaster. They said "chelly" for jelly! Grandma let me stretch the dough for strudels and I could knead bread and roll it out.

My favorite foods were her homemade breads, chicken and *Schupf Nudlas, Halupsie,* strudels, chicken noodle soup, hot German potato

Pheasant sandwiches were served at the canteen at the train depot in Aberdeen to US service members traveling through the South Dakota prairie town during WWII. Aberdeen's Railway Station Canteen opened in 1943, where USO and Red Cross volunteers typically served 500 sandwiches daily. The pheasant meat was donated by hunters. Local businesses also donated to the canteen and residents donated rationed items like butter. By the time the canteen closed in 1946, over 586,000 pheasant sandwiches were served.

salad, bread and butter pickles, pickled beets, and *Kuchen*. She baked date, pinwheel, molasses, and oatmeal cookies. I liked her rhubarb and strawberry jam. She served sausage and we had rice pudding, too. (My mom made that; she was Norwegian). In the mornings for juice I pressed freshly squeezed oranges with an old-fashioned glass. Grandma made a big breakfast of ham, bacon, and eggs when we visited. Grandpa and my dad ate pickled herring and pork hocks, too.

Grandma sewed me an orange gingham dress with ruffled top and skirt that I liked except for the color. Her sewing machine was a black and gold Singer with a pedal and drawers full of colored spools of thread. Grandma made beautiful pheasant hats, too. Each feather was attached separately. In the 1940s and '50s they sold for $45-$50. Hunters and other people bought them in the Aberdeen Pheasant Canteen. One day during WWII, 1,500 troops were served the famous pheasant sandwich and *Kuchen*.

Grandma's pheasant hat forms sat unfinished and ready on a shelf in the basement. Homemade soap and canned foods in the blue jars were lined up on other shelves. When I helped Grandma hold the clothes coming out of the Maytag wringer washer she'd say, "Watch your hair so it doesn't get caught."

Grandpa's woodworking shop was downstairs, too. He kept everything in its place on the bench and hanging from a pegboard. He made me a rocking horse and a chair. They had a laundry chute that I had fun dropping toys and clothes down until Grandma said, "We better go upstairs now. This bag is just muslin and could fall apart."

I'm sure they were tired after I left with all my exploring and questions! One story they always remembered was when I was locked in the bathroom with the skeleton key. I had locked the door so I could look through the tall deep cupboard. Grandma kept saying, "What are you doing in there so long?" When I was ready to come out I couldn't get the door unlocked with the skeleton key so Grandpa had to go outside and climb into the window. I never did see that skeleton key again!

Dad's Auction

Bernelda Kallenberger Becker

W e parked our pickup and travel trailer in front of the *Northwest Blade* newspaper office and crossed the street to enter the Luncheonette café for coffee and *Kuchen*. I had been gorging on the German-Russian delicacy of my childhood every chance I had on this nostalgic trip to Eureka, South Dakota, my hometown, and I had been told I would not be disappointed by the Luncheonette's *Kuchen*.

As I savored the last crumb of my prune *Kuchen*, I said, "Roy, before we leave, I'd like to go into that newspaper office. Maybe I can find the notice of my dad's auction sale in their old newspapers."

"No reason you can't," he said, "but they may not have those old papers anymore." But they did have them, and brought us a large book containing the 1937 *Northwest Blade*. We turned the crisp aged and yellowed pages with great care. I was ready to give up when we reached the September issues. "I must have asked for the wrong year. My old report card showed I was attending school in Detroit that September. The sale would have been in July or August."

"Let's at least keep looking through September and October," my husband replied and kept turning pages. I sighed, convinced we were wasting our time when there, at the bottom left of a page in the September 23 issue, I saw my dad's name. "There it is, Roy. We found it!" I gasped and pointed to the notice. Large bold letters read:

AUCTION SALE

Wednesday, September 29

Rueben Kallenberger, Owner

Embarrassed, I fumbled for a tissue as tears coursed down my cheeks without warning. "I never dreamed I'd have this reaction," I said and began to read. Livestock was listed first.

1 Black Mare, 14 years old, 1 Bay mare, 3 years old, 1 Bay Mare, 5 years old, 2 Bay Suckling Colts. "Dad loved his horses, Roy. When we visited my cousins Floyd and Waldon yesterday, they both mentioned the great pride my father took in caring for them." I sobbed onto my husband's shoulder, imagining the pain Dad must have felt to see his beloved horses on the auction block.

Making an effort at self-control I turned to the manager of the newspaper office and asked if I could get a copy of that page. He allowed us to carry the large book to the local bank across the street where we used their copy machine to make a copy. After we returned the book and thanked the manager, we returned to our pickup. Clutching my treasure to my chest, I wondered what other treasures I'd find if I could take the time to peruse more papers from those years—the years of the Great Depression, dust storms, crop failures, tumbleweeds, and foreclosed mortgages.

Before we left for the trip back to our home in Minneapolis, we purchased *Kuchen* at the local bakery and sausage as only Germans from Russia can make it at Karuk's Meat Market. I wanted to prolong the taste bud memories of my childhood.

As we traveled towards home on Highway 10, we pulled over and stopped four miles east of Eureka for one last look at the farm where I had been born. None of the original buildings remained. "I have so few pictures of those old buildings," I told Roy. "People didn't snap pictures all the time like we do now." There'll come a day our children will treasure their childhood memories in our albums.

Roy pulled out to continue our trip home. I picked up the auction notice and continued reading still surprised that an event held sixty years ago when I was nine years old stirred up so much emotion.

Six milk cows. It sounded so cold—so clinical. They weren't cows; they were bossies—bossies with names. To my surprise, I even remembered some of them. There was Grandma because she plodded along, taking her own sweet time. No hurrying that cow. Jumper had a tendency to find a way to the other side of any fence. And of course, who could forget Kicker. She knocked over many a pail of milk.

I recalled how Mother and I would walk out a ways behind the barn in the evening. She would cup her hands around her mouth. "Owooo owooo owooo" would resound across the rolling hills and usually in response to her call the cows came home for milking. Each cow was a friend. I closed my eyes and relived those hours in the barn—the musty smell of the hay in the mangers, the buzzing of flies, switching tails, three-legged milk stools, and cats—always several barn cats begging for their share.

1 No. 16 DeLaval Cream Separator: What an amazing piece of equipment that had been. Dad would pour the warm milk into the large round bowl at the top, grab the handle, and crank. Out came cream from one spout and skim milk from another. The cream purchased groceries and the skim milk fed the calves. Sixty years later, I drink the skim milk, and I don't know what they do with the cream in our "fat-free" society—even sour cream is now fat-free. I wonder what they feed to the calves now days. I'm now a city slicker and I must confess that I don't know.

Farm Machinery: 1 John Deere Grass Mower, 1 John Deere Plow, 1 John Deere Tractor. Dad was a John Deere man, yes, he was. There was the time Dad went into the house for a moment and left that tractor running. I had my first driving experience on that big old John Deere. Dad caught me just before I hit the barn door at the bottom of the hill.

Household Goods: 1 Kitchen Range. Why didn't they add that it was a Monarch? My mother took great pride in keeping the cooking surface of that range polished to a shiny black. My job, which I hated, was to gather buckets of corncobs from the pigpen to provide fuel for the range.

AUCTION SALE

On my farm located 4 miles east and ¼ mile north of Eureka

Wednesday, Sept. 29

SALE STARTS AT 12 O'CLOCK SHARP

Livestock

1 Purebred Bull
6 Milk Cows
2 Bay Suckling Colts

1 Black Mare, 14 years old
1 Bay Mare, 3 years old
1 Bay Mare, 5 years old

Farm Machinery

1 John Deere Plow, 13-inch
1 John Deere Plow, 14-inch
1 John Deere Tractor, 15-27
1 3-bottum Tractor Plow, 14 in.
   Roller for 3-bottum Plow
2 John Deere Breaker Bottums
1 Grandetour Double Disc, 9-ft.
1 McCormick Grain Binder
1 Deering Corn Binder
1 Emerson Corn Planter
1 1-row Cultivator
1 24-foot Drag
1 Double Disc Van Brunt Seeder
1 26-inch Case Threshing Machine

1 McCormick Header
1 John Deere Grass Mower
1 Moline Hay Rake
1 Hay Rake   1 Buggy
1 Whitte 1½ H. P. Engine
1 No. 16 DeLaval Cream Separator
1 Letz Feed Grinder, 6-inch
1 150-foot Thresher Belt
3 Wagons   1 Header Box
4 Sets Harness
All kinds of tools and many other articles too numerous to mention.

FEED

8 TONS OF CORN FODDER
8 TONS OF STRAW
20 TONS OF GOOD HAY

My FARM
For Sale Or Rent

Household Goods

1 Kitchen Range
1 Perfection Oil Stove
2 Kitchen Tables with 4 Chairs
1 Kitchen Cupboard 1 Sink
1 Dining Room Table, with
  6 Chairs

2 End Tables
2 Beds   1 Child's Bed
1 Rug   1 Dresser
1 Cabinet Sewing Machine
1 Davenport 2 Rocking Chairs

TERMS: Cash or make arrangements with the Clerk Before Sale

Rueben Kallenberger, Owner

Eugene Liedle, Clerk   Willie Heer, Auctioneer

Kallenberger auction sale bill. (Courtesy of Bernelda Kallenberger Becker)

"I can almost smell the bread baking when I think about that stove, Roy. Do you have memories like that, too?" We spent a pleasant half-hour reliving days when we came home from school to big slabs of freshly baked bread, slathered with South Dakota shelter-belt plum jam for me, Wisconsin blueberry jam for him. "I still like to burn my toast," I said. "It reminds me of the burned crusts when the baking loaves touched the sides of the oven."

1 Dining Room Table, with 6 Chairs. I remembered sitting beneath the round oak table, reaching up to the shelf made by the table extenders. Had I taken my Lady Esther cold cream jar, the one I hid my pennies in, from that hiding place under that table before we moved?

1 Cabinet Sewing Machine. Tears welled up again—Mama's Singer. Did she cry when she emptied the drawers of the bits of bias tape, partly used spools of thread, and scraps of overall fabric used for patching? Had those scraps stirred up memories of dresses she had made for me, like the light green one I'd worn to the Christmas program? It had a row of teeny-tiny buttons. I had loved that dress.

I have no memories of that auction day. It was late September. I must have been at the one-room school, probably saying goodbye to my assorted schoolmates. Most of them were cousins. My child's world had no awareness of my parents' pain, their disappointments, and their dreams.

It must have been as painful for my mother to part with useful items she might not have the money to replace as it was for Dad to part with his beloved horses and John Deere equipment—to be replaced by what? They didn't know. They faced a great unknown–leaving South Dakota and all they held dear for the wilds of Detroit, a big city. My father had never done anything but farm. They spoke Low German, knew very little English. My mother's sisters lived in Detroit and had written that jobs could be found there.

I remember blaming my parents for uprooting me from all I loved. Now I know it wasn't a matter of choice—it was necessity. It took sixty years and an impulsive search in a dusty old newspaper to help realize, as I never had before, how they might have felt. In some small measure, after all these years, I now experienced a taste of their pain when the auctioneer's final call, "Sold to the highest bidder," echoed across the farmyard; how they must have felt when the last piece of furniture, loaded on an old truck, disappeared down the driveway, and my father's pain when the last mare and suckling colt were led from the barn.

Previously published in *Good Old Days Specials,* September 1998, and the *Northwest Blade* (Eureka, SD), October 28, 1998.

I Found My Future in Bowdle, South Dakota

Vicki Lynn Kempf Kurle

Bowdle, South Dakota. The unusual name of this little town stuck in my mind since 1959 when I was seven years old. We were on our way to visit my paternal grandparents in Aberdeen, South Dakota, and had a flat tire in Bowdle. My grandparents were in tears when my mom called. They thought we had been at Yellowstone National Park the night of August 17, 1959, when the Hebgen Lake earthquake measuring 7.3 to 7.5 on the Richter scale hit Yellowstone and toppled a mountain. But we got a late start from our home in Boise, Idaho, and were home, safe in bed. However the severe aftershock had awakened us in Boise.

Twelve years later we had moved to Aberdeen. My dad, Joseph C. Kempf, was the administrator of the Bethesda Nursing Home in Aberdeen. He had also leased the Highmore and Bowdle nursing homes. I enrolled in nursing home administration at Presentation College in Aberdeen. Presentation came into existence in 1951. My father's brother, Herbert Kempf, had graduated from Presentation as its first male nurse.

It's spring. School's out, and where do I find myself but living in a rented room in Bowdle, working at the Bowdle nursing home for the summer. Bowdle is sixty miles west of Aberdeen, about a mile square in size—small enough that I can walk anywhere. I don't know anyone. It's my first time away from my family, living on my own. I'm excited and feel liberated, full of anticipation—what will the summer hold?

The 1959 Yellowstone earthquake occurred August 17 at 11:37 pm (MST) in southwestern Montana, measuring over seven on the Richter scale. Also called the Hebgen Lake earthquake, it caused a huge landslide with twenty-eight fatalities and damage over eleven million dollars.

1975 wedding photo of Chuck and Vicki Lynn Kempf Kurle.
(Photo courtesy of Vicki Lynn Kempf Kurle)

That first Sunday morning, I heard church bells from thirteen churches ringing. They were loud. The church of my denomination was close by. Past experience taught me that people in church are kind and friendly. Church would be a good place to get acquainted. I quickly donned my favorite blue-flowered dress and white go-go boots and left for church.

My heart jumped when I walked past one house on my way home from church, and heard someone call out "Hi, Beautiful." A young man

Go-go boots are a low-heeled style of women's fashion boot first introduced in the mid-1960s. They were most often white, low-heeled, mid-calf in height, and made of real or synthetic leather, often worn with miniskirts.

about my age came out the screen door wearing the shortest cut-off jeans I had ever seen and a T-shirt with many holes. He had bushy brown hair and a reddish mustache drooping down on the sides like a horseshoe—the seventies look. Not wanting to be rude, I lingered and we talked for a few minutes before I hurried home.

I became acquainted with other young people at work and in town. To amuse ourselves, we went to the local restaurant, played pool at Harvey's, or played on the swings in the park. I found that in a small town you keep running into just about everyone that lives there, whether you want to or not. It seems everywhere we went, he'd be there.

It was at a local social event that I met Lorraine Kurle, an interesting lady. We became friends. One day she invited me to her home. I was shocked to discover that to enter her home I went through that same screen door that the "Hi, Beautiful" guy had come out of. Lorraine was his mom. His name was Charles—not Chuck, but Charles. By late July he was showing me how to shoot tin cans and gophers. I went with him in the big truck when he delivered equipment for his dad's business. We visited his classmates on local farms. I found out he was a nice guy. I especially enjoyed both his grandmothers— one lived next door and the other lived in their home. I loved joining his large family of aunts and uncles at their gatherings and picnics, so different from my smaller family. Fall came. I returned to Presentation in Aberdeen. Charles returned to his classes at the School of Mines in Rapid City, South Dakota.

The following spring, which of my dad's nursing homes did I pick to work at for my summer job? Bowdle, of course. This time I rented an apartment. I had learned to enjoy many of the ethnic German-Russian dishes

I'd eaten for the first time the preceding summer. I wanted to practice making them. Lorraine gave me some of the local Mothers' Club cookbooks that held those recipes. Charles was home from School of Mines, too. We spent more and more time together. The summer flew by. We were in love!

Forty-two years ago, three days after a twelve-inch April snowstorm, Chuck (Charles) Kurle and I were married in the Bethlehem Lutheran Church in Aberdeen, South Dakota. Through the years our family expanded. Our two sons, Young Chuck and Joseph, married two wonderful daughters-in-law and blessed us with seven precious granddaughters.

Now that we're empty nesters, we have an exciting new hobby: genealogy. All of Chuck's family, my dad, and I have Germans from Russia ancestry. We joined the Germans from Russia Heritage Society based in Bismarck, North Dakota, and the North Star Chapter of Minnesota, one of their local chapters. With help and encouragement from them and friends, we delved into genealogy.

Researching our common ancestry has led to interesting surprises. We have discovered common Germans from Russia ancestors—aunts, uncles, and cousins. They are scattered throughout the adjoining Campbell, Walworth, McPherson, and Edmunds Counties along the North and South Dakota border, and in Dickey and McIntosh Counties in North Dakota. They came from South Russia (now Ukraine) to take advantage of the Homestead Act. So many Germans from Russia settled in this area it was jokingly called the "Rooshin Triangle."

Chuck and I suspect we might be third cousins. I not only found my future, but, as it turns out, also my past in Bowdle, South Dakota.

CHAPTER SIX

One Foot in the Old Country

Salomea Job Dockter, born 1849, Neudorf, South Russia.
Immigrated to Dakota Territory in 1889. Pictured here with youngest child,
Emma, born 1893, Emmons County, North Dakota, circa 1903.
(Photo courtesy of Carol Just)

When a Honeymoon Isn't a Honeymoon

David Delzer

Henry Delzer and Katherine Schock Delzer, circa late 1940s.
(Photo courtesy of David Delzer)

My wife, Linda, and I once stayed with a family in Heredia, Costa Rica. Our host, Sandra, had been born in New Jersey. When her mother and father got married, they told their families they were going on their honeymoon to New Jersey. What they did not share was that it wasn't exactly just a honeymoon. They intended to stay and work, and after eight years they had saved enough to return to Costa Rica and invest in real estate.

This reminded me of my grandfather and grandmother's wedding, just one month before they chose to come to America from Russia. I'm not sure how they decided to get together but it is told that my great-grandfathers Andreas Delzer and Christian Schock met up, shared some alcohol, and decided it would be a good match. So on September 4, 1901, my grandfather Henry Delzer and grandmother Katherine Schock went to the church in New Freudental, and acting as each others' witnesses, they got married in a double ceremony with Katherine's brother and his fiancée. There was a big celebration at the home of Christian Schock with lots of *Kuchen*, wine, whiskey, and dancing. The party may have lasted two or three days.

My great-grandfathers may have also discussed plans to leave Russia. Our German ancestors were upset that the promises made to them by the invitation to settle from Catherine the Great and her grandson Alexander were being set aside. Many of the German settlers were leaving. When my grandfather's youngest brother, Wilhelm, was about to be drafted into the Russian army, both the Delzer and the Schock families decided it was time to leave. Andreas turned his property in Johannestal over to his son, Jakob. Christian sold his property in Helenenthal to another Christian Schock so there was no property transfer to be recorded. The Delzer family, including the newlyweds, left Johannestal in October 1901. They sailed on the *Friesland* from Antwerp to Ellis Island, rode a train to Wishek, North Dakota, and settled in for the winter with relatives.

The trip was harder and took longer for the Schock family and their newlyweds. The extended family headed through Germany to Antwerp. They were held up boarding the ship there because some family members had "sore eyes." When they were well enough to board they headed to New York, but were turned back at Ellis Island because a young family member had sore eyes. The ship's captain took them back on board and dropped them off in Nova Scotia. They took a train west as far as Brandon, Manitoba, and then had to leave the train because they were out of funds. A kind gentleman saw their plight and bought them some bread to eat and purchased tickets for the family to travel to Eureka, South Dakota.

The next summer Christian homesteaded at Maxwell, North Dakota (near Turtle Lake), but lost his homestead to a claim jumper. He then

Trachoma, commonly known as "sore eye," is an infectious disease caused by bacteria. The infection causes a roughening of the inner surface of the eyelids, which can lead to pain in the eyes. In the late nineteenth and early twentieth century, trachoma was the main reason for an immigrant coming through Ellis Island to be deported. Thanks to improved sanitation and overall living conditions, trachoma virtually disappeared from the industrialized world by the 1950s.

bought land in Medicine Hill Township north of Mercer. Great-grandfather Christian was a devout Christian, good natured and humorous, but tall, heavy, and strong, with a temper. He was building a sod house for the family when his wife expressed doubts that he was doing it quite right. He hauled off and walloped the sod wall he had built with his fist and down it came! My father told of a horse Christian had who was acting up. He walloped the horse in the head and it fell over dead.

Families back in Russia lived together and went out from their villages to work the land. When they came to America they filed on homesteads or bought farms some distance from their neighbors. The Delzers and the Schocks ended up miles apart. Both had sons and daughters settling throughout both Dakotas and even into Montana. They all worked hard and made do.

The trip to America must have been daunting just as the immigration into Russia had been. Luckily our ancestors didn't need fancy honeymoons when they were hardy, hard-working, and resourceful individuals who did what they had to do.

The Art of Thumping Watermelons

Matt Klee

While visiting southern Ukraine and Crimea in September 2012 I was struck by the numerous roadside produce stands that were selling dried fish, vegetables, and fruit. Included was an especially delicious variety of yellow melon and sweet round watermelon. I have not been able to find any since then nearly as good in North America.

My grandparents emigrated from Crimea to western North Dakota in 1910 when my father was only a few days old. They brought with them watermelon seeds of the variety they grew in Crimea. I was told that they always planted their watermelons in a patch of virgin soil that they broke up from the prairie sod each year. They would select the watermelon patch based on soil characteristics and drainage and they would never reuse the land for watermelons, preferring to plant in a new location every year. After a few years this led to having the watermelons planted some distance from the farmstead buildings. Of course they saved seeds from year to year but eventually seeds from the original variety were lost.

Fast-forward forty-some odd years to the late 1950s when I was a boy. About once a week, or every other week, the family would get into the 1956 Ford and travel the fifty miles to Dickinson to do the shopping. At the Red Owl, my mom would ask Dad to pick out a watermelon. Dad invariably could pick the best watermelon in the bin. He'd go for the round ones with light and dark green stripes, never those pale green football-shaped ones that came from Texas or some such place.

He "thumped" each watermelon by striking the rind sharply with his finger and listened for the sound it would make. He preferred that method to wrapping his knuckles against the melon. He braced the tip of his middle finger against his thumb and flicked outward against the melon's hide. He

124

Watermelons from Julius Just's *Bashtan* (vine garden) circa 1980s.
(Photo courtesy of Carol Just)

went from watermelon to watermelon, thumping each one, then returned to retest a few before he selected one that was always perfectly ripe and sweet. I'd ask him "Dad, why are you doing that?"

He'd answer, "So I can see if they sound ripe."

"What sound are you looking for?"

"You want a deep hollow sound, not high-pitched and tinny," he'd say. I could not tell one watermelon's sound from the other but I did not argue with his success. I did want to know how he learned his watermelon thumping technique.

In the story he told, it began when he was a boy. He and his two-years-older brother loved the taste of watermelon but they weren't allowed by their parents to go out to the watermelon patch and pick a watermelon to eat. Those melons were to be saved for special occasions and for pickling.

To satisfy their craving for watermelon the brothers would sneak out of the house on a moonlit night and go to a neighbor's watermelon patch, which was often a mile or more away, and help themselves to a melon. They had to perfect the thumping technique so they could pick a melon in the darkness.

"Didn't you ever get caught," I'd ask, and he'd chuckle. "That's why we chose a moonlit night so we didn't trip all over ourselves making a fast getaway."

I never had the occasion to go out at night to thump watermelons, but alas, the art of thumping watermelons has been lost to my generation.

Burian is the Word for Weeds

By Allyn Brosz

The Merriam-Webster dictionary defines a weed as "a plant that is not valued where it is growing." Horticulturists are more succinct: a weed is a plant in the wrong place.

When my great-grandparents arrived from Russia and plowed their first furrows on the mixed-grass prairie biome of their homestead claims in Hutchinson County, Dakota Territory, they disrupted the centuries-long balance of nature and opened the soil to a variety of new species, many of them plants in the wrong place. It took constant vigilance to separate the weeds from the crops. In their first homesteading days, farmers purchased horse-drawn cultivators to keep the weeds under control. Yet less than twenty years after my German from Russia ancestors settled the north-central plains of the United States, legislators in Minnesota and the Dakotas were already considering laws to counter the Russian thistle, which was spreading like wildfire across the newly established croplands, expanding rapidly from the first seeds that stowed away in the flax seeds the immigrants brought with them to the new world in the 1870s. In the 1890s the US Senate Committee on Agriculture established a Russian Thistle Subcommittee. A Minnesota congressman introduced a bill to appropriate one million dollars for the eradication of the Russian thistle, and resistance to this proposal briefly blocked the entire appropriation for the US Department of Agriculture.

My homesteading ancestors fought the weeds year in and year out; when my father took over the Brosz homestead in 1952, he continued the family battle. Throughout fifty years of farming, Dad spent a lot of time ensuring that every plant on his farm was in the right place. His World War II infantry training stood him in good stead in his fight against the green invaders. He patrolled the pastures on foot, armed with a hand-pumped

Russian thistle, also known as tumbleweed, is an invasive weed not native to North America. The invasion is credited to contaminated flax seed brought to South Dakota by German from Russia immigrants in 1873. The weed was widely spread by contaminated seed, threshing crews, railroad cars, and windblown tumbleweeds. By 1900, Russian thistle was found in a dozen Midwestern states and had reached the Pacific Northwest. During the Dust Bowl of the 1930s, when starving animals had little food, Russian thistle "hay" was credited with saving the beef cattle industry.

sprayer or a garden spade to eradicate the Canadian and Mexican thistles that infested the grassland. A few divots were a small price to pay to remove the spiny plants threatening to crowd out the lush grasses that fed his cattle. The roadside ditches were cleared with an occasional controlled burn. To protect the field crops, he rolled out the heavy artillery—tractor-mounted sprayers and field cultivators. At an early age I was drafted into the foot patrol, walking corn and soybean fields to uproot every cocklebur, sandbur, or sunflower that dared to raise its head. Sunflowers were not yet a cash crop in my childhood.

Tough as he was, my father was often fighting a rearguard action against noxious species such as green foxtail, a grass whose sticky green heads clung to our socks. We called it pigeon grass, though I never saw a pigeon near it. I had to step carefully to avoid the sandburs when bringing the cows in from the pasture for evening milking or I'd be picking the prickly pea-sized burs out of my socks forever; I now understand how these plants inspired the invention of Velcro. Wormwood cropped up in the shelterbelt surrounding our farm and it smelled awful! *Schreckliches Wermut!*

Weed wars were not my thing. Pulling weeds in the summer was a hot, sweaty job, and the plants fought back. Deep tap roots wouldn't let go; leaves and stalks stuck and stung; the smelly sap was not pleasant. Go on vacation for a week and you'd have a hard time telling the weeds from the vegetables in Mom's expansive garden. The work didn't end until the first frost.

As a curious farm kid, what intrigued me more than the weeds was that strange word my father used for all the unwanted green stuff. I grew up in a bilingual world and understood the Swabian dialect of my parents and grandparents fairly well, so I could sense my father's unhappiness when he was fighting Mother Nature or discussing weed control measures with his brothers and farm neighbors across the fence row. In his conversations, his mutterings, his occasional cursing, there was one constant: *Burian*. It was *verdammtes Burian* or *zu viel Burian* or *Burian ueberall* ("damned weeds" or "too many weeds" or "weeds everywhere"). By the time *Burian* really registered with me, I was studying high school German in Tripp, South Dakota. *Burian* sounded German—sort of. It fit perfectly in my dad's dialect, but I couldn't find it in my yellow Langenscheidt's paperback German-English dictionary, and consulting the big, black, hardbound Cassell's German-English dictionary on my teacher's desk left me none the wiser. Neither book listed *Burian* under any spelling. I did find out that that the standard German word for weeds is *Unkraut*—literally un-herb or un-cabbage. How strange!

I finally turned to my German teacher "Duane Schrag" for help. His roots are German from Russia, too. He grew up in Freeman, South Dakota, a community settled by Mennonites, Hutterites, and Swiss Volhynians, and a language teacher, too, so he was very familiar with the local dialects. He patiently explained that languages aren't static; they are shaped by the environment in which their speakers live. When my ancestors left the Black Forest, some aspects of their everyday language did ossify; their eighteenth-century Swabian retained its lovely, drawling lilt throughout their sojourns in South Prussia and Bessarabia. But in all their wanderings, my German ancestors lived among people who spoke Polish or Russian, so it was only natural that they would borrow or adopt some of the most common words of everyday discourse that they heard the natives speak. Linguists call these "loan words." My ancestors spoke this spiced Swabian in steerage, crossing the Atlantic, and it echoed across the Dakota prairies as they worked together to build their first houses from the prairie sod.

Finally! Now I grasped the idea that my father was speaking Russian! *Burian* was the Russian word for weeds. My German from Russia ancestors listened to their neighbors bemoaning the constant battle with *Burian* and they began to use that word for their weed struggles, too. This was confirmed by the German travel writer, historian, and geographer Johann Georg Kohl. Traveling through the Russian steppes in the 1830s, shortly after my ancestors arrived there, Kohl made this observation:

> One of the first words that a stranger learns in the steppe is *burian*. The constant topic of the farmer's lamentation is *burian*; and the gardener, the herdsman, and the herd, join with equal bitterness in heaping malediction on the detested *burian*. The curiosity of every new arriver is, therefore, soon excited by an expression of such constant occurrence, and after some inquiry he finds that every plant or herb... from which [the cattle] turn away, is ruthlessly classed in the condemned list of *burian*. (Kohl 1844, 473)[1]

After giving it some thought, I discovered that *burian*, like other exotic words of the farmyard and the kitchen, such as *Gatsche* or *Kaczka* (ducks), *Halupsie* (stuffed cabbage rolls), borscht (vegetable soup*)*, and *Plachinda* (pumpkin turnovers), glinted in my ancestors' dialect, hinting at the Polish forests and Russian steppes where they had once lived, far from their Black Forest homeland. I think of these words as linguistic markers, similar to the strands of cellular DNA that reveal my ancestral origins. But by the time my great-grandparents reached America and settled on the prairies, those words were no longer on loan; they were fully embedded in the structure of their everyday speech. The American prairie was now my ancestors' world; their dialect was the unique speech of the Germans from Russia, and these words, borrowed from Polish and Russian, were faint ghostly echoes, recalling the *Heimats* they had left long ago.

[1] Johann Georg Kohl, *Russia: St. Petersburg, Moscow, Kharkoff, Riga, Odessa, the German Provinces on the Baltic, the Steppes, the Crimea, and the Interior of the Empire* (London: Chapman and Hall, 1844.

The Prairie Blacksmith

Merv Rennich

The vast majority of the Germans from Russia who immigrated to the United States were farmers who worked hard to "tame" the prairie and make the land productive. Their success depended on the use of tools and implements made of metal or metal parts. A plow pulled by horses was very ineffective if the plowshare was broken or dull. Likewise other equipment like the harrow, the sickle mower, and the reaper needed frequent repair. Thus the foundation craft of blacksmithing was an essential part of the farming community for repairing, mending, sharpening, and creating the tools and implements as necessary for the farm to be successful.

My grandfather Karl Rennich Sr. was a blacksmith. He was a big man and he pounded and shaped hot iron for over forty years from the time he was an early teenager working in his father's blacksmith shop on the treeless steppe of South Russia until he died, fashioning the hot metal in his own shop on the treeless prairie steppe of central North Dakota.

His first business, in the Reformed village of Waterloo, Beresan District, South Russia (now Stavky, Ukraine), grew to include a wagon factory that had seven employees. He was inducted into the Czar's army and fought the Japanese in Manchuria. Not long after Russia's defeat, he returned to Waterloo and to his business. However, he was constantly afraid he would be inducted into the army again. That, along with the general political unrest at the time and the stories of others who immigrated to America, prompted him to make a decision. So he, his wife, Christina, and their three children (including my father) left the rest of their family and immigrated to America in 1909 where they settled in the small village of Mercer, North Dakota, located sixty miles north of the state capital, Bismarck. In Mercer he bought a blacksmith shop and again built his business. He became widely known and respected around the area as a master blacksmith who could make or repair anything made of iron.

A story printed on the front page of the local weekly newspaper, the *Mercer Telegram*, dated August 4, 1911, relates how a wealthy Dr. Heinzeroth was taking his family to Brush Lake, a popular weekend retreat two miles north of Mercer. They were driving a fancy new Pierce-Arrow automobile, a luxury car that cost several thousand dollars (a lot of money back then). Several miles from Mercer the car broke down and was towed behind a lumber wagon to my grandfather's blacksmith shop where it was discovered that the rear axle was broken into two pieces. Grandfather told the doctor that he did not know if he could fix it or not, and since it was Saturday, it wouldn't be until well into the next week at the soonest that a new axle could possibly be obtained from Bismarck. Before he could say anymore, the doctor wanted to know if there was a car available for him to buy or rent. There were none, as most of the townspeople were already at the lake for the weekend.

The doctor was very upset and desperate. Here he was stranded with his family and a broken-down car. He muttered, "I should have never bought this car!" Then Grandfather thought a bit and said to the doctor, "I will trade my Model T Ford, which is in good working order plus $100 for your broken Pierce-Arrow." The doctor thought over what my grandfather said and then replied, "It's a deal!" The two men shook hands and the doctor put his family and things into the Model T and left for the lake. The used Model T was worth about $400.

That night, after other work in the shop was under control, my grandfather decided to see if the axle could be repaired or if they had to wait for a replacement. It was a clean break midway between the wheel bearing journal and the spline end that connected to the differential. Since the forge was still hot he decided to give it a try. With my father helping, he took the failed axle pieces to the hot coals where they worked past midnight welding the red-hot iron back together using a hammer and anvil. This was not a

One of seven wrought iron crosses in the Zion Lutheran Cemetery,
Mercer, North Dakota, created by blacksmith Karl Rennich.
(Photo courtesy of Merv Rennich)

normal blacksmith job as it required very precise work so that the axle retained
its original dimensions and shape, a difficult requirement for forge welding.

The next morning, the repaired axle was installed in the car. It was
Sunday. Grandfather put his family (my grandmother, my dad, my aunt, and
my uncle) in the Pierce-Arrow with the top down and motored to Brush Lake
for the rest of the day. At the lake they tooted the horn, smiled, and waved as
they drove past the surprised doctor and his family. This was a family story
that was told many, many times over during the ensuing years.

Another story about my grandfather tells about his artistic
blacksmithing ability to make iron crosses. Seven children of one family in
the village had died either shortly after birth or as youngsters. The children's

father came to the blacksmith shop and asked Karl if he could fashion an iron cross to put over the children's graves. Karl obliged. In his spare time when not fixing machinery, he made iron crosses of his own design using scrap iron. An iron cross was placed over each grave. In all, seven crosses were made and placed in the Zion Lutheran Church Cemetery six miles south of Mercer, North Dakota.

The crosses were made using only the forge, the hammer, and the anvil. There were no welds, screws, bolts, or cast pieces. Holes were made without using a drill and the pieces were held together using hot iron clips or rivets. Karl's design was unique. He was one of the very few non-Catholic wrought iron cross makers. Some seventy years later, on October 23, 1989, because of the iron crosses made by my grandfather, the United States Department of the Interior placed the Zion Lutheran Cemetery on the National Register of Historic Places.

Karl's career as an accomplished and creative blacksmith left a legacy. His son was a widely known farm equipment master mechanic. His grandson was the first college student and engineering graduate in the family. Three of his great-grandsons are engineers and his great-great-grandson is an architect.

CHAPTER SEVEN

Schnapps Anyone?

(Photo courtesy of Carol Just)

What We Choose to Remember

Mel Meier

I t's amazing what one's mind chooses to remember over a lifetime. Much of my upbringing was in the 1950s and 1960s. There are events we all remember like where we were when President John F. Kennedy was assassinated and what we were doing when the events of September 11, 2001, unfolded.

I grew up on a farm near Napoleon, North Dakota, the Logan County seat, located in south-central North Dakota. A large percentage of the Logan County population was settled by Germans from Russia from the Black Sea area of South Russia. My paternal great-grandfather immigrated to the United States in 1911 from Rosenthal, South Russia. My maternal

Sgt. Andrew J. Leier, US Army Air Force, 1943. (Photo courtesy of Mel Meier)

great-grandfather immigrated to the United States in 1885 from Mannheim, Russia. My maternal grandfather's last name was Leier. His father, my maternal great-grandfather, immigrated to the United States in 1889 from Elsass, Russia.

One memory in particular left a big impression on my young mind. My uncle Andy, my mother's brother, fought in WWII and was killed on October 7, 1944. The family had to wait until June 14, 1949, before the Armed Forces sent my uncle's remains to the family for burial. But first a wake was held. In those days wakes were held in the homes, a practice that lasted until the late 1950s and early '60s. I sat on my dad's lap in the *Stupe* (living room) of my grandparents' house. The flag-draped casket, with large lit candles stationed on either side of it, created a somber and dreary mood. I remember having a tremendous feeling of sadness.

The next day I stood next to my grieving parents as we watched the approaching hearse escorted by uniformed members of the Armed Forces. They buried Uncle Andy in his final resting place, the cemetery next to the small rural St. Boniface Catholic Church where Uncle Andy grew up. I knew my maternal grandparents until they passed away in the 1980s. Never once in all that time did I hear my Uncle Andy's name mentioned. Part of their Germans from Russia heritage was to internalize their emotions.

Our Catholic community practiced celebrating *Namenstag* or your Names Day. Certain days of the year in the Catholic Church are assigned to the memory of certain saints. The Feast of St. Stephen is on December 26. My dad's name was Steve so we had a wild and busy three days—Christmas Eve, Christmas Day, culminating with my dad's Names Day on the twenty-sixth. We had as many as fifty people show up at our home for this occasion. Of course card games of pinochle and whist were played. Lunch was served for everyone, with plenty of ring sausage, sandwiches, and *Kuchen* on hand. I wonder if anyone celebrates Names Days anymore.

One could never tell the story of German from Russia life without emphasizing the importance of music. In the Catholic tradition in which

Schnapps or schnaps is an alcoholic beverage that can be made with distilled fruit brandies, herbal liquers, infusions, or flavored liqueurs added to neutral grain spirits. Schnapps (English spelling) is derived from *Schnaps*, colloquial German related to the term *schnappen*, referring to the practice of consuming the drink in a quick slug from a small glass.

I was raised, many of the hymns at Sunday Mass were sung in German. Christmas midnight mass was not complete without singing "Stille Nacht." There were joyful German songs sung at weddings and sad songs ("Das Schicksal") sung at funerals. An example of this type of funeral is seen in the 1960s movie *Dr. Zhivago*.

Polka dancing has been one of the great experiences of my lifetime. My mother taught me to dance at an early age and I have continued dancing all my life. The importance and significance of the accordion as an instrument to bring our traditional music to life cannot be overestimated. The popular rise of Lawrence Welk brought our German from Russia music to the national stage. He was one of our own and he was proud to promote our music. On the local level, wedding dances were a weekly affair and accordion bands sprang up all over to play at these events. Accordion playing still exists today as is evidenced by North Star Chapter member and lifelong friend Steve Weninger.

Hochzheit schnapps (wedding whiskey) was another German from Russia custom. Many people mixed the schnapps themselves. It's a combination of 190-proof alcohol and heated sugar water. To make this you certainly needed to know what you were doing. You would see this schnapps at wedding receptions. There was a person, *ein Schenker*, which translated is a "pourer," stationed on either side of the reception hall door with a bottle of schnapps. As the guests entered the hall each adult was offered a "shot" of schnapps. The guests would then continue into the hall (once they got their breath back). *Hochzeit* schnapps was used on other occasions like anniversaries and birthdays. I remember my grandfather giving us grandkids a "taste" on every Christmas Eve.

When I was growing up, churches (no matter what denomination) were more than places of worship. They were the centers of social activity. My 4H club met at the church. Youth groups met at the church. Some churches hosted polka and square dances. On Sunday afternoons you could usually find a softball game at your church. Many of the games were between neighboring churches in the area. Community was all important. When one parishioner rejoiced the entire church community rejoiced. When one parishioner grieved they all grieved. As time went on, one by one the churches closed. The sense of community and closeness disappeared along with them.

I observed many ethnic practices as a youth. One of them was the practice of *Brauche*. I was about ten or eleven years old when my dad woke me up one night and told me to get dressed. My parents could not get my one-year-old sister to stop crying. We drove to the home of an elderly lady in Napoleon. I remember her home as dark and eerie, almost to the point of being scary. There were lit candles and the lady said some prayers over my sister. She then gently moved my sister's limbs back and forth to relieve her stomach pain. Almost immediately, my sister fell asleep and slept all the way home. I was totally impressed by the entire experience. I later discovered that there were others who practiced *Brauche,* especially for children who contracted ringworm.

As I mentioned before, community was very important to the Germans from Russia of our small town of Napoleon. There was no better example than what I experienced as the "Great Saturday Night Get-Together." No matter how hard you worked during the day, when Saturday evening came along, almost everyone got cleaned up and headed for "town." Now Napoleon was a rather sleepy and unassuming town during the week, but on Saturday night Napoleon came ALIVE. Main Street was packed with people walking back and forth. Bumper-to-bumper cars tried to navigate through the mass of people. Two movies played at the show hall and the four beer joints were packed.

Mel Meier dancing with his mother, Margaret Leier Meier, on the occasion of
her 80th birthday, circa 2006. (Photo courtesy of Mel Meier)

My great-uncle Chris (Christian) Leier owned the Coast-to-Coast
store. People clustered together all over the store catching up on the latest
news. People stocking up their weekly provisions kept the four grocery stores
busy. Before people went home, they usually visited the restaurant for a
burger, or the White Maid (Napoleon's version of a Dairy Queen) for a hot
fudge sundae. One of the few businesses that has withstood time and still
exists today is the White Maid. The Saturday night get-togethers died out in
the 1960s. Memories are all that is left of that time.

A staple mark of our German from Russia life was the cuisine. I
must say I was very lucky. I knew my mother for almost seventy years and
she never served a bad meal. She loved cooking and it showed. My dad had a

---

Rivel is an egg drop soup that has many variations in ingredients, spelling, and pronunciation, depending on the German dialect and region.

"sweet tooth." She always had something sweet to eat like cake, cookies and/ or *Kuchen*, chased down with a piece of ring sausage.

We worked in the fields all day, and dinner, the big noon meal, supplied energy. Foods based in flour and other starchy foods, high in carbohydrates (energy), ruled the day. They included dumplings, *Dampf* noodles, *Fleischkuechle*, *Rivel* soup, and potatoes. Supper was our lightest meal—soup, sandwiches, chicken, sausage. There was always dessert—pie, chocolate cake, or who could ever forget *Kuchen*. *Kuchen* is a pastry made out of a dough shell with custard filling. There were as many versions of *Kuchen* as there were women baking them. One thing was consistent though— everything was goooood!

Meat was also important. Most farmers butchered their own livestock for beef, pork, and chicken products. Before we had a freezer we took the meat to the locker plant in town. They packaged it and stored it in their freezer. Once we got our own freezer the locker plant processed it and wrapped it, and then we could store it ourselves. As I got older, every year I helped my mother butcher chickens. My mom and I had kind of an assembly line going. The most chickens I can remember butchering in one day was thirty.

Time and progress march on but memories do not. Memories are windows through which we catch a glimpse of what made us who we are. I am eternally grateful for my memories.

Childhood Memories of Celebrations

Henrietta Weigel

Weddings

Weddings were simple but very special occasions in my community, Zeeland, North Dakota. They were not elaborate events; they were more like big family get-togethers. We assumed all family and friends would be there if they had been invited. Because people generally stayed in the same area in those days, there was no need for guests to travel long distances like they do now. Children weren't usually invited unless they were part of the immediate family so when my parents, Joseph G. Weigel and Elizabeth Therese (Malsam) Weigel, were invited to a friend or cousin's wedding, I was excited and honored to attend. After I was old enough, I was asked to help serve food, clean tables, and wash and dry the dishes. It made me feel I was part of the wedding instead of staying at home as I had before.

Brides wore simple white gowns they purchased through the Montgomery Ward catalog or in a bigger city like Aberdeen or Bismarck. Bridesmaids all wore the same dresses in spring colors, but not necessarily color-coordinated with any kind of color theme. The bride's bouquet was often made of flowers from the garden or handmade from wood-fiber paper.

Weddings were all-day celebrations and lasted past midnight. Because of strict religious rules in our Catholic church, they were held on Tuesdays or Wednesdays. If they carried over into Fridays we weren't allowed to eat meat, and Sundays were considered days of rest. The day before the wedding, the bride's family and friends prepared food and set up tables for the big day. The wedding mass was at ten o'clock in the morning. A noon meal and a reception followed at the Zeeland City Hall. Food was served family style; we passed the bowls around from guest to guest. Tables were

Dish towels: a typical wedding gift in the 1950s

(Photo courtesy of Carol Just)

loaded with chicken noodle soup, mashed potatoes with gravy, chicken, beef, coleslaw, Jell-O salad, corn, bread, milk, coffee, and wedding cake for dessert.

To make room for dancing, tables were shoved to outer walls after the meal. The band played waltzes, fox trots, and polkas on the accordion and harmonicas. They sang "Beer Barrel Polka," "The Blue Skirt Rose," "You Are My Sunshine," "My Wild Irish Rose," and many others. Watching was fun; however, we didn't join in the dancing unless they played the butterfly or the bunny hop, because they were easy to learn and one didn't need a partner. Even though our mother was a good dancer, she had never taken the time to teach us how to waltz or polka. At about six o'clock in the evening, the dancing stopped. The tables were pulled back out from the walls so sandwiches and leftovers from the noon meal could be served. After this, most guests went home to do evening chores and freshen up while the rest of us washed dishes and put tables back into storage. Meanwhile, the bride and groom opened their gifts with a few people watching, probably family and wedding attendants. Gifts were usually practical things like pillowcases and flour-sack dish towels embroidered with flowers or the days of the week, crocheted doilies, decorative glass bowls, Pyrex pie and cake dishes, and glass pitchers with matching glasses.

About nine o'clock people returned from doing their chores, and friends and neighbors who hadn't been at the wedding came to join the fun. The band took their place, and the bride and groom danced their first dance together. Then the bride and her father danced, along with the groom and his mother. Next the wedding party would exchange partners and dance, and finally the guests could join in. To dance with the bride or groom people paid a dollar. Everyone had fun visiting, dancing, and drinking too much homemade wedding schnapps.

Christmas

Christmas was plain and simple in my childhood. We treated it like a typical Sunday, a day of rest when only necessary chores were done. We always went to midnight mass on Christmas Eve. Most years we didn't get any gifts because money was scarce. One very special year, my sister, Kathy, and I got Catholic Sunday missals as Christmas gifts. In the missals, all the Latin prayers were translated to English. We were thrilled to have our own so we could follow along with the priest, praying the traditional Latin prayers like everyone else.

Christmas dinner was goose or duck with mashed potatoes and gravy, homemade bread, and corn, with chocolate pie for dessert. Ma made special candy: fudge made with cocoa, cream, sugar, vanilla, and water or divinity, made out of egg whites, sugar, and vanilla. She made the best divinity; she wasn't very good at making fudge. She also bought a variety of hard candies that were only available at Christmas time, such as ribbon candy and peanut brittle.

Since the economy wasn't very good after World War II ended, things available to buy as Christmas gifts were limited. There were many Christmases when we didn't exchange gifts at all. People that did purchase Christmas gifts did their shopping from the Sears, Roebuck or Montgomery Ward catalogs. Christmas catalogs with special clothes and toys began arriving in our mailbox about ten to fifteen years after WWII. My younger brothers, John and David, began getting toys for Christmas in the mid-1960s, and they were metal trucks. I think they were more durable and much better quality than the mass-produced plastic trucks available for children now.

In our house we had an artificial Christmas tree, about twelve to eighteen inches tall, with electric bubbling glass candles. It wasn't customary for people in the farming communities of our area to decorate the house with lights or tinsel.

Winter Visiting and Other Entertainments

Henrietta Weigel

Farm people enjoyed visiting friends and neighbors during the winter. It was the time of the year when, after chores, they met in each other's homes to play card games like pinochle and whist. We children could go with our parents if the home they were visiting also had children, but I don't remember it happening very often. Of course, living in North Dakota, the weather affected plans, too. Dad usually let the car engine run five to ten minutes to warm it up and get the windshield defrosted. Plans quickly changed when the temperature was too cold for the car to start.

Two or three times a year, we would visit our Weigel grandparents and Ma's sisters in Aberdeen, South Dakota, which was a two-and-a-half-hour trip. We got up at five thirty in the morning to do the chores and have

Zeeland City Hall. Placed on the National Register of Historic Places in 2017.
(Photo courtesy of Tom Isern)

breakfast before we left at seven o'clock. Grandpa, dressed in his Sunday suit and tie, met us at the door with a whiskey bottle in one hand and a shot glass in the other. For a welcome drink, he served us schnapps. It was a homemade mixture of sugar, browned in a pan on the stove, water, and 190-proof Everclear grain alcohol. It was strong! One tiny sip felt like it burned all the way down to your big toe.

Grandma always cooked potato sausage for the noon meal because it was one of Dad's favorite meals. Ma, my sister, Kathy, and I didn't like the smell or taste of the sausage casing, so Grandma cooked meat and potatoes for us in another kettle. After helping Grandma wash the dishes, Ma, Kathy, and I went downtown to shop for new dresses at a store called Three Sisters. Sometimes we visited one of Ma's sisters, Katie, Annie, or Agnes. We had to leave for home by four o'clock or four thirty in the afternoon because chores were always waiting for us when we got home.

We also went to Bismarck, North Dakota, a few times to visit one of Dad's brothers, Eugene, and his wife, Anne, and their children, our cousins Donald, Rodney, and Shirley. It was the custom to show up at one another's houses unannounced because none of us had telephones. Visitors were always welcome; food was in the refrigerator and doors were unlocked. Nobody worried about break-ins. Ma usually brought meat and eggs to contribute to a meal.

Our cousin Shirley had received Roy Rogers and Lennon Sisters paper dolls as a gift. They were new to Kathy and me, and we had lots of fun playing with them. When we were at home, we came up with the creative idea to design our own paper dolls using the Sears, Roebuck and Montgomery Ward catalogs. The catalogs had men, women, and children, dressed in work, dress, and play clothes. We cut these out of the catalogs with scissors to dress our paper dolls. The paper dolls didn't look as nice as Shirley's and the clothes didn't fit very well, but we didn't care. We knew Ma and Dad would never buy anything so frivolous for us to play with. At our mother's funeral, years later, while talking with our cousin Mert about life on the farm, she mentioned how she and her sisters always enjoyed playing with our catalog paper dolls when they visited us.

By the late 1950s, farmers in the area were able to buy telephones and have them installed. Then it was possible to communicate plans to visit and to keep in touch more easily. All the phones were set up as party lines that connected five to seven families. When the phone rang, it would ring on every phone that was connected to the party line. Each family was set up to have a designated amount of rings for an incoming call. There was no privacy because you knew who was getting the call and everyone connected to the party line could listen in and respond if they wanted to. We didn't have a telephone in our home when they first became available, but it was a new technology that brought changes to the community.

Movies were black and white. Colored movies and television weren't available in our area until the mid-1950s. Once in a while we went to a show featuring the Three Stooges, Dean Martin and Jerry Lewis, or Amos and Andy at the Zeeland City Hall. We sat on folding chairs. No popcorn, candy, or soft drinks were sold. The movie was projected onto a white background by a movie reel machine. It ran on a sprocket rolling from one reel to another. Occasionally, the movie flickered and stopped because the film came off the sprocket. We heard the projector running in the background, making a clicking sound. The picture on the screen moved forward slowly and looked choppy. Sound effects were very simple and came from a small speaker in the projector. In a rural area like ours, movies weren't a huge priority and we didn't need to update equipment in order to have fun. On a summer evening, we sometimes drove thirty miles to Linton to watch a movie at the drive-in theater. Dad parked our car in a stall next to a speaker attached to a pole. We had to leave the car window open to hear the movie. Now drive-in theaters are mostly a thing of the past.

Looking back, I can see how much things have changed. Now we keep our doors locked, and we carry our own personal phones and can be reached anywhere at any time. We call friends and family in advance to plan visits because most people have very busy schedules. For movies, we don't have to leave the house if we don't want to. Our cars are much better for getting around whenever we want and we have the option of calling a cab to drive us places. In all, these improvements have made it easier to stay in touch with others and enjoy a variety of entertainment events.

Afterword

The Immigrants' Heritage

Kristine Lamp

They came, then more came,
Seeking refuge and promise
To a land unknown, a land of freedom.
Farewells meant heartbreak, the journey hard,
But determination prodded their souls
For release from bondage, from oppression,
Though the cost be great, the goal greater.
They came for land, for their future
To serve God and family
And the generations to follow.

They came, they persevered, they won,
Despite the sacrifices, the lacks,
Harsh weather, poor crops, loneliness.
Undaunted, they worshipped God
Thanking Him for provision,
Leaving a heritage for children
And children's children's children
To remember their vision, why they came.
Knowing sacrifice, toil, and hardship
Gave them this treasure, this heritage
That though life can be hard,
The past gives us strength
To face our own tomorrows.

Author Bios

Bernelda Kallenberger Becker was born in Eureka, South Dakota. Interest in her heritage began with an article in the *Star Tribune* about the 1996 American Historical Society of Germans from Russia (AHSGR) convention in Bloomington, Minnesota. Attending it launched Bernie into unearthing her rich and interesting heritage. She joined the North Star Chapter of Minnesota and discovered their library, the AHSGR and Germans from Russia Heritage Society (GRHS) archives, and new friends. Retired, Bernie writes for Christian publications and secular magazines. Her ancestral villages are Neuberg, Kassel, and Güldendorf.

William (Bill) Bosch grew up in Emmons County, North Dakota. After graduating from Linton High School he attended North Dakota State University and the University of Nebraska-Lincoln. After completing his PhD he taught mathematics at the University of Northern Colorado. He has published two books on German-Russian history: *The German-Russians in Words and Pictures* and *Russian Agriculture in the 1880s*. He lives in Spearfish, South Dakota, with his wife, Margaret, and daughter, Julie.

Allyn Brosz grew up on the Hutchinson County, South Dakota, farm homesteaded by his great-grandfather Adam Brosz, a Bessarabian German. His mother's family came from the Glückstal colonies. Allyn attended a one-room country school, graduated from Tripp (SD) High School, and earned a BA *cum laude* in government and a master's in public administration from the University of South Dakota. He completed a Fulbright study year at the University of Saarland in Germany, earned an MA in political science from the University of Oklahoma, and completed graduate studies at the Johns Hopkins University School of Advanced International Studies Bologna Center in Italy. As a child Allyn spent time hanging out with the old folks, absorbing their stories of the old country told in a lilting Swabian dialect. Those stories sparked his lifelong interest in his German from Russia heritage.

Sharon (Grenz) Chmielarz was born and raised in Mobridge, South Dakota. She graduated from the University of Minnesota and taught German and English. She has had eleven books of poetry published including her latest, *little eternities* (2017). Her work has been a finalist in the Midwest Book Awards, the Next Generation Indie Book Awards, the National Poetry Series, and has been nominated often for a Pushcart Prize. Among her awards are the New Rivers Voices Award and the Jane Kenyon Poetry Award. Her father, born in a sod house, was a Grenz from the Fredonia, North Dakota, area. You can hear her read poems at www.sharonchmielarz.com.

David Delzer grew up on the prairie near Douglas, North Dakota, the oldest of eight children who all worked hard to make the Delzer farm a success. He graduated from North Dakota State University with a degree in mechanical engineering. David retired from the Minneapolis VA after twenty-four years as facilities maintenance manager. He serves on the Richfield (MN) Friendship City Commission and is a Medicare counselor for Senior Community Services. He enjoys square dancing and traveling. His German from Russia grandparents came from Ukraine in 1901.

Nancy Gertner grew up on a farm in Cottonwood County, Minnesota, with two older sisters, a farmer father, and a teacher mother. Her Gärtner great-grandparents emigrated from the Grunau District of the Black Sea area in 1876. After completing a degree at Minnesota State University, Mankato, Nancy joined the Navy and ran off to see the world. Following her Navy retirement, Nancy returned to Minnesota and married Paul, an Army guy. Nancy volunteers with several organizations and is the owner of the Shady Nook one-room schoolhouse that three generations of her family attended in Cottonwood County. With Paul's help, Nancy continues to restore the Victorian-era school.

James Gessele is a native North Dakotan of German from Russia descent. He received his BA from Concordia College, Moorhead, Minnesota, and MAT in German from Stanford University. After a career in teaching, including a four-year stint teaching English in a German grammar school, he entered civil engineering and retired in 2001 when he took up translating as a hobby. Two of his works have been published; several more are in development. He has served as editor of the Germans from Russia Heritage Society's quarterly, *Heritage Review*.

Carol Just was born and raised in Berlin, LaMoure County, North Dakota. She has researched her family history since she was a teenager. She is an oral historian with a degree in pioneer and Native American women's history. All of her great-grandparents emigrated from the Glückstal Colonies and Bessarabia in South Russia in the 1870s and 1880s. Carol has traveled to her ancestral villages in Ukraine, Bessarabia, Germany, Alsace, and Poland. She is a charter member of the North Star Chapter of Minnesota Germans from Russia.

Matt Klee grew up in Halliday, North Dakota. He holds a bachelor's degree in nuclear engineering from the University of Virginia. He worked for thirty-eight years at the Xcel Energy Prairie Island Nuclear Generating Plant and is now retired. Matt is a member of the Germans from Russia Heritage Society and currently serves as spokesperson and webmaster for the Crimea Regional Interest Group.

Larry Kleingartner was born in 1945 in south-central North Dakota to a first-generation German from Russia family. He was raised on a farm and attended a one-room rural school until fourth grade. He played basketball at Bismarck State College and the University of Jamestown. Upon graduating from the University of Jamestown he joined the Peace Corps and spent two years in rural India working with tribal people to improve their agriculture.

He received a master's degree from the University of Hawaii. He spent most of his professional life working for the National Sunflower Association. Larry currently serves on the Board of Directors for the Germans from Russia Heritage Society and the Western Synod of the Evangelical Lutheran Church in America.

Charles (Chuck) Kurle grew up in Bowdle, South Dakota, and graduated from the South Dakota School of Mines and Technology with a bachelor's degree in mechanical engineering. He became interested in genealogy when his son and daughter-in-law gave him a historical research document on the Kurle name that said his grandfather Jacob was the first recorded Kurle to land at Ellis Island. Chuck and his wife, Vicki, have two married sons and seven granddaughters. He enjoys genealogy, fishing, and woodworking.

Vicki Lynn Kempf Kurle was born in Aberdeen, South Dakota, and grew up in Idaho. Her Kempf ancestors were among the founding families in Bessarabia in 1816. They immigrated to Ashley, North Dakota, in the late 1800s. Her grandmother was born in 1899 in Hillsview, South Dakota, where the Schmidt/Krein/Will ancestors settled. In 2009 Vicki saw her relatives on a Germans from Russia website and learned about the North Star Chapter of Minnesota. Vicki likes genealogy, cross-stitching, fishing, and cooking. Her ancestral villages are Neudorf, Marienberg, and Glückstal. Vicki and her husband, Chuck, have two married sons and seven granddaughters.

Kristine Lamp lives in Savage, Minnesota, and has authored the books *Dogs Just Make Life Better*, *The Life and Times of Clarice Rew*, and *My Companion – Sometimes Hidden, Always There*. For her church, she has made devotional booklets including one for Lent and one for Advent as well as a book of poetry. Currently Kris is working on a historical novel about the German pioneers from Russia. It amazes her how the generations have so diligently preserved their heritage.

Duane Maas (1939-2016), a long-time North Star Chapter member, grew up on a farm near Jamestown, North Dakota. He was proud of his German from Russia heritage, descending from the village of Kassel, South Russia. He graduated from North Dakota State University with a master's degree in mathematics and began his teaching career in math and German in rural North Dakota, finishing his career as a math professor at Minnesota State University, Mankato. In between teaching endeavors, Duane worked as a computer software engineer with Sperry Univac, Control Data, and Lockheed Martin. With his brother Gene, Duane made several trips to Germany for ancestral research, finding distant relatives.

Paul Maggitti grew up in Baltimore County, Maryland. He earned a bachelor's degree in rural sociology from North Carolina State University and was a Signal Corps Officer in the United States Army. He received a master's degree from the Naval Postgraduate School in Monterey, California. Following retirement from the Army, Paul married a farmer's daughter and moved to Minnesota, where he worked for a defense contractor before retiring to collect toy trains.

Mel Meier grew up in Napoleon, North Dakota. After attending grade school in the local school district, Mel attended St. John's University and Seminary in Collegeville, Minnesota. In 1970 Mel left seminary and for the next three years worked in the Twin Cities as a religious education coordinator. In 1973 Mel began a thirty-four-year career with Northwest Airlines as a transportation agent and eventually agent supervisor at Minneapolis/St. Paul International Airport. Now retired, he resides in Burnsville, Minnesota. Mel's paternal grandparents and maternal great-grandparents emigrated from German villages in Kutschurgan and Crimea regions in South Russia.

Cynthia Miller was born in 1969 and grew up in Beulah, North Dakota, surrounded by her Black Sea German heritage. She holds bachelor's degrees in mass communications and political science from Minnesota State University Moorhead and a master's degree in journalism from Iowa State University. Her thesis was a study of German-language newspapers in the Midwest published for German from Russia immigrants. She has worked in communications in several fields, freelances as a writer and speaker, and volunteers with Girl Scouts. She lives in the Twin Cities with her husband, Sean, and children, Gustave and Susanna.

Virginia "Ginny" Weispfenning Peterson's parents' families emigrated from the Besserabia region on the Black Sea. They settled in the towns of Kulm and Fredonia in south-central North Dakota. After high school in neighboring Ellendale, Ginny left for Minneapolis to further her quest to become an artist and art teacher. She attended Bethel University and the University of St. Thomas, graduating from the University of Minnesota. In the span of her artistic career Ginny produced a number of paintings she called *Horizon*, expressing contemporary themes of the Dakota landscapes. She is retired.

Merv Rennich grew up in McClusky, North Dakota. He attended the University of North Dakota then worked for Caterpillar Tractor Company with various overseas assignments. Merv's father was born in Waterloo, Cherson District, South Russia, and came to the United States in 1909. Merv's mother's family came from Hoffnungstal, Bessarabia, in 1903, all settling in Mercer, North Dakota. Retired, Merv enjoys playing in a German polka band, doing genealogy research, writing, traveling, and visiting grandchildren.

Ron Scherbenski grew up on a farm near Eureka, South Dakota. He attended Westmar College in LeMars, Iowa, and graduated from Dunwoody College in Minneapolis. He married Pamela Miller of Minneapolis in 1965 and has lived in St. Louis Park, Minnesota, since 1970. Ron and Pam have two children and two grandchildren. Vacations were spent traveling to all fifty states and twenty-one countries. Since retiring in 2006, they have continued to travel and Ron enjoys tinkering with cars.

Lillian (Lil) Kleingartner Ward is the youngest of ten children raised on a farm south of Gackle, North Dakota. Her father, Balzer Kleingartner, was born in 1900 in Hoffnungstal, Bessarabia, and came to America with his family in 1902. Lil's mother's (Martha Miller) family came from Neudorf, Glückstal Colony, South Russia. Lil and her husband, Dayton, spent their careers in the Minneapolis area and raised three daughters. After retirement, Lil and Dayton began traveling, including a memorable 1999 trip to Germany where they met a first cousin's family and discovered second cousins. Lil and Dayton have been members of the North Star Chapter of Minnesota since 1999.

Henrietta Weigel was born on a farm near Hillsview, South Dakota. She spent most of her childhood on a farm north of Zeeland, North Dakota, and attended a one-room school for grades one through eight. Her long (forty-two years) career was spent with Cargill in Minnetonka, Minnesota. Now retired, she lives in Bloomington, Minnesota. Henrietta says, "A big accomplishment for me was getting used to living in the big city and learning how to swim after I retired."

Kathy Weigel was born in Eureka, South Dakota, but grew up on a farm north of Zeeland, North Dakota. She attended a one-room country school from grades one through seven. For grades eight through twelve she attended school in Zeeland. Kathy moved to Minneapolis in 1967 where she was employed with Cargill. Kathy is now retired and lives in Bloomington, Minnesota.

Louise Wiens was born in Göttingen, Germany, in 1955 and immigrated to Leamington, Ontario, with her parents at the age of five. Her mother, from Leipzig, Bessarabia, was exiled to Siberia in 1945. Her father, from Kleefeld, Ukraine, was exiled to Siberia in 1942. This is where they met and married. As a semi-retired nurse, Louise now has more time to write, including a regular column for a local publication as well as a column for the Germans from Russia Heritage Society *Heritage Review*. Louise visited her ancestral villages in Bessarabia in 2015. She is married with two grown children and a husband who is not interested in history.